D0515479

WITHDRAWN
UTSA LIBRARIES

RESOURCE BOOKS FOR TEACHERS

series editor

ALAN MALEY

PROJECT WORK

Diana L Fried-Booth

Oxford University Press 1986

Oxford University Press
Walton Street, Oxford OX2 6DP

Oxford   New York   Toronto
Delhi   Bombay   Calcutta   Madras   Karachi
Petaling Jaya   Singapore   Hong Kong   Tokyo
Nairobi   Dar es Salaam   Cape Town
Melbourne   Auckland

and associated companies in
Beirut   Berlin   Ibadan   Nicosia

Oxford is a trade mark of Oxford University Press

ISBN 0 19 437092 5

© Oxford University Press 1986

All rights reserved. No part of this publication may be
reproduced, stored in a retrieval system, or transmitted, in any
form or by any means, electronic, mechanical, photocopying,
recording, or otherwise, without the prior permission of
Oxford University Press.

This book is sold subject to the condition that it shall not,
by way of trade or otherwise, be lent, re-sold, hired or otherwise
circulated without the publisher's prior consent in any form of
binding or cover other than that in which it is published and
without a similar condition including this condition being
imposed on the subsequent purchaser.

Set by Katerprint Co. Ltd, Oxford

Printed in Great Britain at The Alden Press, Oxford

LIBRARY
The University of Texas
at San Antonio

Acknowledgements

I am grateful to the Bell Educational Trust for granting me a sabbatical term in order to embark on writing *Project Work*. I am also deeply indebted to Richard Rossner; without his encouragement, trenchant advice and influence, this book would not have materialized. Furthermore, I wish to acknowledge all the students and overseas teachers of English who have worked with me both at the Bell School of Languages in Bath and on courses abroad and whose enthusiastic co-operation and interest have been instrumental in developing the ideas put forward in the book. Finally my thanks go to my husband, Howard, who has provided constant moral support and tolerated endless discussions with my students often into the small hours with unfailing good humour and patience.

Acknowledgements are also made to:

Oxfam, for the use of their leaflet *Build Your Own Shanty House*.

Francesca Brotto, for the extract in Appendix II, published in *Problems and Experiences in the Teaching of English*, by La Nuova Italia and Oxford University Press, Volume II No. 2, 1985, and to Karen Delbarre, Heloisa Medeiros, Marja Rohio, Heidelies Müller, Gerd Gaupass, Zorica Stojilović, and Beate Vogel for examples of projects also in Appendix II.

Contents

The author and series editor

After graduating, DIANA L FRIED-BOOTH taught English in Ghana, returning to take up a research assistant's post in Rural Communications at Reading University. She has worked in the West Midlands on language resource centres in primary schools, and integration schemes for immigrants in the secondary sector. She joined the Bell Educational Trust in 1976, where she was involved with teacher training and directing the pre-sessional courses at Bath. As a freelance teacher trainer she works on short courses for The British Council in Europe and is a chief examiner and author for the Cambridge TEFL examinations, involved with examination construction and development at a variety of levels.

ALAN MALEY has worked for The British Council as English Language Officer in Yugoslavia, Ghana, Italy, France and China. He is now Regional Representative for The British Council in South India (Madras), from where he coordinates the Council's English studies programme in India. He is particularly involved with teacher training and distance education.

He wrote *Quartet* (with Françoise Grellet and Wim Welsing, OUP 1982). He has also written *Beyond Words*, *Sounds Interesting*, *Sounds Intriguing*, *Words*, *Variations on a Theme*, and *Drama Techniques in Language Learning* (all with Alan Duff), *The Mind's Eye* (with Françoise Grellet and Alan Duff), and *Learning to Listen* and *Poem into Poem* (with Sandra Moulding).

Foreword

This book makes an important contribution to three areas of the continuing debate in TEFL/TESL: authenticity, learner autonomy, and motivation.

Much of the discussion on authenticity has been tiresomely unproductive. Yet, in the carrying through of a project, at least four types of authenticity are necessarily present:
- authenticity of language input
- authenticity of task
- authenticity of event
- authenticity of learner experience.
Project work also provides one solution to the problem of learner-autonomy, of making the learner responsible for his own learning. By its very nature, project work places the responsibility on the students, both as individuals and as members of a co-operative learning group. Autonomy becomes a fact of life.

It seems likely that the authentic 'feel' of project work and the fact that the learners are brought face to face with their own learning, are important factors in the high levels of motivation observable in project-centred activities.

No one, least of all the author, would claim that project work offers some kind of magical remedy to all our problems in TEFL/TESL. Nor even that this book is the final word on projects.

However, this is the first attempt to bring together into a coherent presentation the wealth of practical know-how on the subject. For this reason alone it will be a welcome addition to the literature. And it should appeal equally to classroom teachers and to trainee teachers.

Alan Maley

Introduction

About project work

In this brief Introduction, I shall give an outline of the aim and nature of project work, its function in a language teaching programme, the way in which projects are developed, and some of the difficulties which may be encountered.

First, however, I should like to offer a few general thoughts on language learning and, in particular, student motivation.

Most organized language learning takes place in the classroom. What is taught in the classroom may in theory be useful, but the usefulness does not always extend to practice. Often, there is a gap between the language the students are taught and the language they in fact require. It is this gap that project work can help to bridge.

Recent approaches to language learning and teaching (particularly those broadly termed 'humanistic') stress the importance of co-operation among learners as a motivating factor. Such approaches (e.g. Community Language Learning) focus not only on interpersonal relationships but also on the involvement and development of the individual. The more fully the student is involved in an exercise, the more likely he or she is to see the work through to the end, and to benefit from it.

It is this sense of personal involvement that gives the impetus to project work. For the students, the motivation comes from within not from without. The project is theirs. They themselves decide (in consultation with the teacher) what they will do and how they will do it, and this includes not only the content of the project, but also the language requirements.

Since the project is student-centred rather than teacher-directed, the teacher may need to develop a more flexible attitude towards the students' work. The project is not designed to suit a syllabus, and the language required derives not from the textbook but from the nature of the project itself. However, the project must first be planned and discussed, and later evaluated. And it is here that the teacher can provide valuable assistance. Much of this language work takes place in the safe, controlled environment of the classroom, where the teacher is on hand to help the students gain linguistic confidence. She is also there to help solve the problems that will inevitably arise once the project moves out of the classroom into the world.

A project moves through three stages: beginning in the classroom, moving out into the world, and returning to the classroom. At each of these three stages, the teacher will be working *with* the students, not directing them but acting as counsellor and consultant—and, in this way, enabling them to take a project of their own devising out of the classroom into the world.

Defining a project

It may be useful at this stage to distinguish between the two main elements of this book: *full-scale projects* and *bridging* or *motivating activities*.

These are, of course, closely linked, since the motivating activities (e.g. redesigning the front page of a newspaper, Chapter 1) are a form of preparation for full-scale projects. The main difference between the two is that motivating activities are restricted to the classroom, while project work is extended beyond the classroom.

A full-scale project involves three stages. These are:

1 *Classroom planning.* The students, in collaboration with the teacher, discuss the content and scope of their project, and predict their specific language needs. Ideas are also discussed for projected interviews, visits, and for ways of gathering necessary material— pamphlets, brochures, illustrations, etc.

2 *Carrying out the project.* The students now move out of the classroom to perform whatever tasks they have planned, e.g. conducting interviews, making recordings, gathering printed and visual material. It is important to remember that at this stage they will be using *all four skills*—reading, writing, speaking, and listening—in a naturally integrated way.

3 *Reviewing and monitoring the work.* This includes discussions and feedback sessions, both during and after the project. Advice and comment offered by the teacher, group analysis of the work, and self-monitoring by the participants (see Chapter 3 *The project in action*).

Students differ, not only in their interests but also in their language needs. A full-scale project may not always satisfy their immediate requirements. It is important, therefore, that they should have access to other activities, which do not necessarily involve all four skills and which do not need to be extended beyond the classroom. These are the *bridging* or *motivating activities*.

Below is a short list of some of the bridging activities to be found in this book. The order of presentation is an approximate guide to the simplicity or complexity of each activity and to the level of linguistic control:

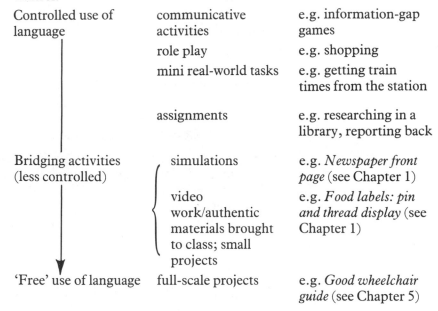

Controlled use of language	communicative activities	e.g. information-gap games
	role play	e.g. shopping
	mini real-world tasks	e.g. getting train times from the station
	assignments	e.g. researching in a library, reporting back
Bridging activities (less controlled)	simulations	e.g. *Newspaper front page* (see Chapter 1)
	video work/authentic materials brought to class; small projects	e.g. *Food labels: pin and thread display* (see Chapter 1)
'Free' use of language	full-scale projects	e.g. *Good wheelchair guide* (see Chapter 5)

For further ideas, see especially Chapter 1 (Bridging strategies) and Chapter 5 (Case studies).

The advantages of project work

By encouraging students to move out of the classroom and into the world, project work helps to bridge the gap between language study and language use. It is, therefore, a valuable means of extending the communicative skills acquired in the classroom.

Much language learning operates through tasks devised by the teacher, to which the students are expected to respond; that is:
– Teacher defines language → Students practise language and task

In project work, by contrast, the students become responsible for their own learning. They select and devise the project, with the teacher acting as co-ordinator and 'facilitator' or consultant, i.e.
– Students devise task → Language needs evolve from task; students refer to teacher when necessary

This is the difference between motivation which comes from without and motivation which comes from within. For a balanced teaching programme, both approaches are needed.

Language learning does not always progress at a steady and predictable pace. Great advances may be made by the beginner, but at intermediate level the student often reaches a 'plateau', from which there is little incentive to move on. It is at this crucial point in learning—the *intermediate level*—that project work can offer the much-needed incentive.

The motivation lies in the project itself. The student is—at last—offered the opportunity of using the language skills already acquired, in a situation which is new, challenging, and real. The project draws not only on the familiar and the predictable, but also on the unfamiliar and the unpredictable. This is the incentive to 'go on' from the plateau to the next slope.

Clearly, if students are to carry out project work they must have some command of the target language. But this need not mean that it should be restricted to intermediate and advanced students. There are many projects involving work outside the classroom which can be tackled by students with only an elementary knowledge of the language.

Project work and the language skills

In addition to its motivating power, project work also provides a useful way of integrating the four skills in what I have described as the *layered approach*. By this I mean the development of language skills, not imposed from without but arising naturally from within, and developing cumulatively in response to a basic objective, namely, the project.

The need for a given skill does not occur in a fixed order relative to the other skills. A particular skill may be practised individually, but this does not mean that it is separate from the others. In project work the skills are not treated in isolation, but combined.

In the initial stages of a project— stimulus, discussion, negotiation— there may be more speaking and listening than reading and writing (though something a student has *read* may well spark off discussion). Once the project is under way, however, the students will be using all four skills simultaneously. Speaking and listening (e.g. in the interviews), writing (taking notes), and reading (brochures, pamphlets, background material)—in short, combining the skills.

Different projects, of course, require different procedures. And so different skills will come into prominence at different stages. For instance, *Third World display* (Chapter 5) outlines a project based on Third World issues. Here, the students need to *read* before they can talk on the topic. By contrast, the *Good wheelchair guide* (Chapter 5), clearly requires *discussion* and exchange of ideas before the students begin to read or write.

Finally, although project work does not impose upon the students a fixed language pattern to be followed, it does offer them the opportunity of practising in the classroom the language they are likely to require outside. The *Primary school teaching* project (Chapter 5), for example, outlines a project in which students undertake to teach small groups of children in a primary school. Before any teaching can take place, the students must first visit the school, introduce themselves to the staff and to the children. In this case, the language needed for formal introductions can be practised in the classroom before the students go out on the project. Similarly, the *Expedition task* and *Street interviews* (Chapter 5) describe projects in which students have to conduct street interviews. In the classroom, the students can usefully practise the functions they are most likely to need, e.g. apologizing for disturbance, interrupting politely, etc.

For a more detailed illustration of the way in which the language skills can be interrelated in a project, see Chapter 1: *How do you make an English apple tart?*

Developing a project

For a project to succeed, a good working relationship needs to be established. The students must be able to co-operate not only with each other but also with the teacher. Groups who are accustomed to student-centred activities will find project work an extension of a familiar approach, rather than an innovation. Those who are used to more formal, structured teaching methods may need to be introduced first to the bridging activities (Chapter 1), which are specifically designed to develop receptiveness to project work.

The length of time spent on a project will, clearly, depend on the amount of time available, and on the nature of the project. For this reason, I have opted for a flexible approach which will allow groups to work at their own speed, according to their own needs. The projects outlined in Chapter 5, for instance, could take as little as three hours or as long as twelve weeks to complete. And each project can be shortened or lengthened according to need.

But, however long or short the project may be, it will pass through certain stages of development. These are:

1 *Stimulus*. Initial discussion of the idea—comment and suggestion. The main language skills involved: speaking and listening, with possible reference to prior reading.

2 *Definition of the project objective*. Discussion, negotiation, suggestion, and argument. The longer the total time available for the project, the more detailed this phase will be. Main language skills: speaking and listening, probably with some note-taking.

3 *Practice of language skills.* This includes the language the students feel is needed for the initial stage of the project, e.g. for data collection. It also introduces a variety of language functions, e.g. introductions, suggestions, asking for information, etc., and may involve any or all of the four skills (particularly writing, in the form of note-taking).

4 *Design of written materials.* Questionnaires, maps, grids, etc., required for data collection. Reading and writing skills will be prominent here.

5 *Group activities.* Designed to gather information. Students may work individually, in pairs or in small groups, inside or outside the classroom. Their tasks will include conducting interviews or surveys, and gathering facts. All four skills are likely to be needed.

6 *Collating information.* Probably in groups, in the classroom. Reading of notes, explanation of visual material, e.g. graphs. Emphasis on discussion.

7 *Organization of materials.* Developing the end-product of the project. Discussion, negotiation, reading for cross-reference and verification. The main skill practised, however, will be writing.

8 *Final presentation.* The manner of presentation will depend largely on the form of the end product—chart, booklet, video display or oral presentation—and on the manner of demonstration. The main skill required is likely to be speaking, but could be backed up by other skills.

This scheme can, of course, be adapted to suit the requirements of individual projects.

Using projects in a non-English environment

A teacher working in an environment where English is spoken as the mother tongue has the advantage of being able to send the students out into a world where the language they need is, literally, on the doorstep. In such circumstances, the long-term project presents no difficulty. Teacher and students can improvise as the project progresses, knowing that access to the target language is guaranteed.

A teacher working in a non-English-speaking environment, however, does not have this advantage, and therefore cannot ask the students to embark upon a project without having made preliminary arrangements.

This is a discrepancy which must be recognized, and which I should not like to discount. Nevertheless, my experience suggests that it is not so much the language environment that matters as the sense of motivation and commitment to the project. (Reference is made in Appendix II to various projects being developed by teachers in non-English-speaking environments.)

English is an international medium of communication. In most countries there will be useful sources of language material which students (and teachers) should be encouraged to tap. Embassies, consulates, travel agents, banks, large department stores—all offer ready-made material in English. (More detailed suggestions are given in Appendix I.)

To summarize: it is not necessary to live in an English-speaking country in order to carry out a project. It is not the environment that determines the success of a project, but the students' motivation. The material can be found, if one is willing to look for it.

Possible problems

In spite of all the progress that has been made in language research, we still do not know how people learn and, particularly, how the language of the classroom is absorbed and later put to use outside the classroom.

Project work offers the student an opportunity to put into practice what has been learnt through formal teaching. That is, it takes the experience of the classroom out into the world. It puts teaching to the test. And, most importantly, it provides an opportunity for informal as opposed to formal learning.

The benefit for the student is clear: he or she is working on a topic of interest and is using language for a specific purpose, with a particular aim in mind. What has already been learnt can now be put to use, and what else is needed can be learnt.

But for the teacher, the project may incur certain problems. These are:

1 *Organization*. Projects do create extra work. The teacher may already find it difficult to keep up with regular lesson planning and with the preparation and marking involved. Projects require an additional commitment, e.g. in establishing contacts, finding suitable sources for material, etc.

2 *Monitoring*. Students using language outside the classroom need a teacher to keep track of what they are doing. This means that strategies have to be devised for checking systematically on what the student has heard, learnt, and understood. And, of course, what he or she may have *said* while conducting the project.

Some of the burden of monitoring can be shifted onto the students themselves, by providing checklists (e.g. for new vocabulary, idiomatic expressions, etc.) and project report forms. (For fuller details, see Chapter 3.) Where available, audio and video recording equipment can also be used to help in assessing the students' performance.

3 *Personal problems*. The teacher needs to be ready to help the students deal with difficulties such as the following, which may arise at any stage of the project. Lack of interest or motivation among certain

members of the group; a general loss of motivation resulting from 'overkill', i.e. too intense a pace during the early stages of the project; fear of being unable to cope with the new language demands; disappointment with specific features of the work, e.g. unsuccessful interviews. These problems are dealt with in detail in Chapter 3.

I should like to conclude, however, on a positive note. Problems and difficulties do exist, but they must be seen in the right perspective. The considerable advantages of project work more than compensate for the occasional difficulties which may arise and for the additional work which may be required of the teacher, particularly in a full-scale project.

Finally, I should like to stress the immense benefit of project work, both to students and to teachers. The students' motivation begins with their personal investment in the project. This motivation is sustained and increased as the work progresses. Firstly, because it affords them the opportunity to practise in the classroom the language for which they themselves have seen the need. Secondly, because the project enables them to use the target language in real situations. Thirdly, because in most cases it leads to tangible results—an end product which they themselves have created. And lastly, because it leads to a deepening of personal relationships—so difficult to achieve in day-to-day classroom work—between teacher and students and among the students themselves.

In this book the pronouns 'she', 'her', 'hers' are used to refer to the 'teacher'.

1 Bridging strategies

The use of bridging activities

Teachers who want to incorporate project work into their teaching will need to introduce their students gradually to the idea of student-centred language work. There is a list of suggested bridging activities in the Introduction. In this chapter there are more detailed descriptions of useful communicative activities. The length of time spent on such bridging activities, and the range covered, will obviously depend on each individual teaching situation, and how used students are to working on their own, and performing communicative activities.

Most teachers will already employ various techniques which encourage their learners to experience and use language as authentically as possible.

There can be few teachers who do not make use of role play and other similar techniques, ranging from semi-scripted and prepared dialogues, through guided situations, right to totally authentic, free use of the foreign language. Such activities are useful at all levels of achievement. Similarly, many teachers nowadays are familiar with and make use of a variety of communicative activities which can again be graded in terms of freedom of student input. A rather controlled activity of this kind is the 'branching conversation' where the dialogue is supplied in the form of a flow chart with alternative answers possible. The students choose which parts to use and thus build up their own dialogue. For example:

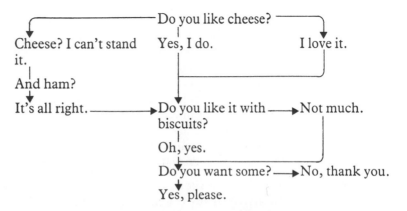

where the situation is given but the students choose their own words. A freer version of this, where students are concentrating not on what they say for its own sake, but are using the language to achieve an aim, is in so-called information-gap activities. A classic example of this is where two students each have a map, but neither has all the details. The aim is to find a hidden treasure, but first the safe route has to be established by means of information gained from the partner or opponent.

If you are working in an English-speaking environment, your students will be exposed to authentic language stimuli all the time. It is therefore a relatively straightforward procedure for them to perform 'mini real-world tasks' (see Introduction) and assignments, and to collect authentic data, e.g. to buy newspapers, to listen to the radio, to watch a TV programme or to put a question to an English person such as their landlady. Teachers working outside the UK will almost certainly have to build up a small resources centre within the classroom (see also Chapter 2 on organizing a project) so that the students have instant access to data collection. At some stage, however, you are going to want your students to go outside the classroom and you will want to discover how your students react to working outside the classroom and what problems you as a teacher may encounter.

As a starting point you could consider using a simulation such as Ken Jones's 'Radio Covingham' (*Nine Graded Simulations*, 1974). In some situations it may even be possible for students to follow this with a visit to a local radio station. In this case perhaps only two students should carry out the visit, and then report back to the group. The whole class, however, can prepare questions for a visit, and the answers can be edited to form a classroom broadsheet. If you work in a big city or a tourist area, for example, in a non-English speaking country, you may find there is a radio station near you where there are some English-language broadcasts.

A similar exercise might use one of the *Geography games* (published by Longman, 1973), for example, 'Breadline'. You and your students can discuss ways in which the initial task of the simulation can be further extended.

You may be able to organize a visit to an exhibition, a museum, or a relief agency headquarters, or to get a guest speaker, film, or slide show within the classroom. Any of these activities could be used to extend the language to genuinely communicative interaction. There could be students from developing countries in your own class or at your school or college, or else studying at your local college, polytechnic, or university; there could be immigrants or refugees settled in the vicinity, and establishing contact with any of these people will encourage your students to see how the language generated within the classroom lends itself to activities outside.

Your initial reaction to this suggestion might be one of doubt or misgiving; many teachers feel that their students simply will not be able to cope with the level of language required. In my experience students at an intermediate level upwards respond well to a situation which pitches them into a real language environment. They appreciate the confidence placed in them by the teacher, their self-esteem is enhanced way beyond the degree to which it can be enhanced by the classroom role play, and the teacher/student relationship benefits likewise.

It's Your Choice, by M Lynch (published by Edward Arnold, 1977), a series of role play exercises designed for secondary school native speakers, also provides ideal material for adaptation as a bridging activity. The themes cover a variety of topical subjects, for example, motorway planning, pop festivals, street violence. If you get a positive response to any one of these topics you can move towards the follow-up stage; an outside visit may not always be practicable or desirable, but it may be possible to invite a guest speaker or another group of students for a debate or a discussion, a seminar, or a workshop session. If you have access to video or audio-recording equipment you might try recording part of these follow-up activities and using the recordings for further classroom discussion of specific language items. The main objective will be to ease your students gradually away from a teacher-centred approach to a situation where they have an increasing say in what they do.

In trying out any of these activities you will need to encourage the students to try and express their own language needs. If they want to invite a guest speaker, what language items do they need in order to do so? Allow pairs of students to itemize their language needs before trying to reach a group consensus, but make sure that the students realize that if you go on to teach the language relating to a formal invitation, it is because they have asked you to do so.

Be alert to ways of exploiting any situation for extended language work which demonstrates clearly how all the skills can be incorporated. A simple request made by some students may be an ideal means for setting up a framework which would both bring together the classroom and the outside world, and at the same time bring together the four skills.

The following example illustrates the potential generated by such a request during a two-week summer course. The request was quite simply, *How do you make an English apple tart?*

1 How do you make an English apple tart?

<u>**LEVEL**</u>   **Intermediate to Advanced**

<u>**AGE**</u>   **Adolescent upwards** (though much of it could be covered by linguistically advanced juniors)

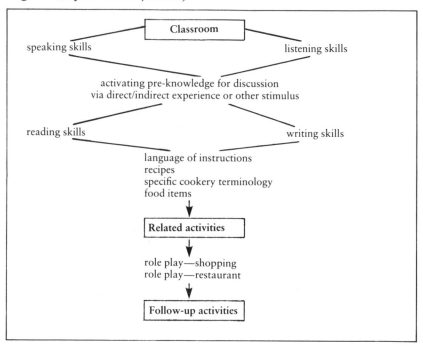

<u>**PROCEDURE**</u>   1 Start by comparing the eating habits of people in the UK, with those of your students.

2 Compare the price of food and its availability.

3 You can discuss with your students the differences between national and regional dishes.

4 If practicable, have a demonstration cookery lesson, entertaining the other teachers and students to a tasting session.

5 Your students can cook their own national dish(es).

6 Ask your students, in pairs, to prepare a recipe booklet of English recipes to take home with them.

7 You can take your students on a group visit to a supermarket, market or specialist food shop(s).

8 Take your students on a group visit to a restaurant, or a food-processing firm.

<u>**COMMENTS**</u>   Obviously some of these activities involve the use of a kitchen and incur extra costs; you must select what is appropriate for your own situation. The object of this breakdown is to show the potential behind a simple request.

2 Food labels: pin and thread display

LEVEL   **Elementary to Intermediate**

AGE   **Junior to Adolescent**

PROCEDURE

1 Ask your students, for example, what they eat, what they ate yesterday, what food they like.

2 Your students should volunteer the information, leading to a discussion, translation or structural practice. Use the blackboard if appropriate.

3 Ask your students where the food comes from, e.g. spaghetti from Italy, apples from France, biscuits from Germany, etc.

4 Home-based task: ask your students to collect as many food labels or wrappings as possible from cartons, tins, packets, jars, bottles, etc., over a period of, for example, one week.

5 Divide the class into groups to produce a world outline map for wall display purposes, using plain paper and felt-tip pens (see Figure 1.1).

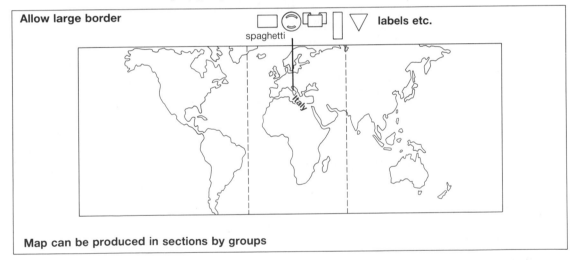

Figure 1.1

6 Get your students to bring their labels, etc., to the lesson. Ask questions such as:
– *What have you got, Juan?*
– *I've got a chocolate wrapper from Switzerland.*
You can then ask whether any other students have anything from Switzerland. Individual students can take responsibility for different countries and collect labels. When a pattern has been established the students can ask the questions so that the information gathering process is student-directed.

7 At this point the activity can be developed in a number of ways. It is likely that certain countries will predominate, depending on the trading position of the students' own country or environment. Using an atlas if necessary, the students can locate within the world outline all the countries which get a mention and have an accompanying label.

8 If possible different coloured pins with matching thread can be used to link items and their country of origin, e.g. a red pin and thread for Italy, a green pin and thread for France, etc. If no coloured pins are available, use plain pins with coloured thread which is usually easily available and cheap. Attach the thread to the pin and stick the pin into the country; draw the thread taut and secure it with another pin on the border or margin of the world map by the name of the food item or the label, depending on the numbers involved. Otherwise the labels can be used to decorate the border of the map. If there are only a few items, food names could be written on the map itself.

9 The completed map can be exploited orally. The students can talk about the countries for which they had responsibility, the products coming from these countries, etc., the map can be used as a stimulus for written work; a controlled or guided exercise, report writing, or free writing.

COMMENTS

This activity generates spontaneous language practice. In my experience some students pursue the home task on their own initiative and actually go to shops and supermarkets in order to buy extra items. A healthy rivalry can develop over who can collect the most labels and who has labels which no one else has. All the students are involved irrespective of language ability.

The exercise is easy to set up and involves little additional cost. It provides a permanent classroom display and the stimulus for further language work can be exploited on an individualized basis.

3 Pocket-money survey/personal budget

LEVEL

Intermediate

AGE

Junior to Adolescent

PROCEDURE

1 Start by saying to the whole class, for example:
– *When I was your age I used to get 50p* (or equivalent in local currency) *a week pocket-money, how much do you get?*
Encourage a general discussion. Then ask individual students, for example:
– *What do you spend your pocket-money on?*
Your students contribute their own personal information. This stage can be exploited for work on comparatives, if appropriate.

2 Either you or one of your students can write the information on the blackboard (see Figure 1.2).

Sum of money	Number of students	Items money is spent on
50p	𝗟𝗛𝗧 11	sweets
60p–75p	𝗟𝗛𝗧 1111	comics
80p–£1.00	𝗟𝗛𝗧 𝗟𝗛𝗧 11	cinema
£1–£1.50	𝗟𝗛𝗧 111	football
over £1.50	11	swimming
no pocket-money	1	ice-cream
		savings
Total number in class: 47		

Figure 1.2

3 Go on to ask your students the following questions, e.g.
– *What do your brothers or sisters get?*
– *What do your friends get?*
– *What do the students in class 4 get?*
– *What do you think the average figure might be?*
– *Let's find out for sure, how can we find out?*
The students make suggestions, and hopefully, someone will suggest a questionnaire. Otherwise you should suggest this. (Note: this is a suggested sequence of questions—others may be more appropriate.)

4 Ask your students to look at the sample questionnaire, and in pairs, discuss possible questions and format for their own questionnaires. The whole class can then put together a list of items for the final questionnaire.

5 In groups, ask the students to work on the questionnaire design (see Figure 1.3), and ask them to suggest what the final questionnaire might look like.

6 When agreement has been reached on the questionnaire format by the whole class, arrange for it to be reproduced. If reproduction facilities are unavailable, each student can be asked to make five copies, or whatever number is required.

7 If necessary role-play the interviews in the class to establish that your students have the appropriate language they require to conduct the survey. Allow the students two nights/one week, or whatever is desirable, in order for them to interview the required number of other students.

8 Oral feedback, informal discussion: discuss with your class how the information is to be collated, for example, in the form of a graph, block diagram, or by pasting the questionnaires on the wall.

9 The final result can be exploited for written purposes, report, and summary writing, guided written practice on comparatives or superlatives.

Secondary School Student
Name: ....   Age: ....   Class: ....
Total pocket-money received Sweets and ice-cream Comics and magazines Cinema Football Swimming Clothes Savings

Figure 1.3

You may make photocopies of this page for classroom use (but please note that copyright law does not normally permit multiple copying of published material).

COMMENTS

This exercise takes the language outside the classroom in a fairly controlled form which does not require monitoring. It generates potential for varied language practice. There are no hidden extras to the exercise and it is straightforward to administer. In my experience, students identify very readily with the subject and, moreover, it can be adapted for higher language levels or adults. You may have to reassure adults, however, as they might not want their personal financial situations revealed. They could invent figures. Here is a sample form for adults.

Adult
Name
Total weekly/monthly expenditure Rent/mortgage Food Transport Clothes Newspapers Gas/electricity Entertainment

Figure 1.4

You may make photocopies of this page for classroom use (but please note that copyright law does not normally permit multiple copying of published material).

4 Staff portrait gallery

LEVEL

Intermediate

AGE

Adolescent (possibly young adult)

PROCEDURE

1 In a large school, especially at the beginning of a new school year, many of the new students will not know who the staff are, and new staff will be unknown to everyone. This could provide a starting point for discussion over how the situation could be remedied, but the idea is not restricted to any particular time and is just as useful at the start of a short course. After an initial discussion you can show your students a personality page from a newspaper, magazine, or brochure to illustrate the idea of format.

2 Ask the students what they already know about individual staff, i.e.
– Title: Ms/Mrs/Miss/Mr/Dr
– Role within the school: Head of Department
– Subject(s) taught
– Outside interests, etc.

3 Then with the whole class construct a list of all or some of the staff depending on what is relevant. Ancillary, secretarial, and catering staff can also be included.

4 Ask students to select staff to photograph or sketch, interview, and write a brief impression of.

5 Make sure you warn staff in advance of requests for interviews, photographs, etc.

6 With the whole class draw up a timetable to allocate which students will take a photograph, sketch, or interview. The opportunities for doing these will vary from school to school and the overall sense of staff co-operation with the activity; it should be stressed that only a few minutes are required with each individual.

7 You should agree with your students on questions to ask (see step 2 above). This activity can be done in pairs or on a gaming basis. Other questions to ask could include:
– *How long have you been teaching at this school?*
– *What do you do in the holidays?*
– *What is your favourite TV programme?* etc.

8 Allow a period of time for students to carry out the assignments and then collate the information. If the material is going to form a permanent or semi-permanent display, you will need large sheets of fairly stiff paper. This can be prepared in advance, and might look something like the illustration in Figure 1.5.

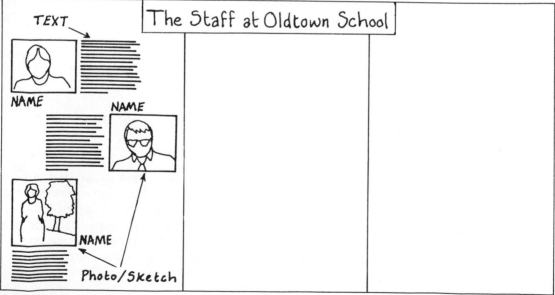

Figure 1.5

9 Oral practice: ask your students to exchange information. Direct and indirect speech can be exploited here.

10 Written texts can be prepared to accompany the sketch or photograph. The following is a suggested model: *This is Kurt Wiedermann. He teaches chemistry and has been here for six years. He is married with two children and plays the guitar in his spare time.* The written text will reflect the language level of the students; the oral practice session should enable the students to write up their texts with the minimum of teacher intervention.

11 A broadsheet can be compiled and displayed.

COMMENTS

This exercise also takes the language outside the classroom in a fairly controlled form with no monitoring role for the teacher. It employs all the skills, and produces a useful end product with advantages for students outside the group who actually produced it.

Note that if a camera is available (a polaroid is ideal), cost will have to be considered. Otherwise, it is possible to rely on pencil sketches or even photos supplied by staff.

5 Team-work exchange skills

LEVEL

Intermediate to Advanced (depending on difficulty of reading text)

AGE

Adolescent upwards

PREPARATION

This project is best performed with two classes and two teachers. Otherwise, one class is divided into two groups, each having a text. In any case, two teachers are needed.

The success of this activity depends on the choice of reading texts. The two texts need to be of approximately equal length and difficulty, and contain sufficient material to promote discussion and query. The one essential requirement is for two rooms, preferably adjacent or close to each other, otherwise co-ordination over the exchange of students necessitates a runner, who is usually the teacher.

PROCEDURE

1 Ask each group to read their text individually.

2 Ask one member of the group to open a discussion on the text, to establish the gist, vocabulary, etc.

3 Ask one of the students to write on the board a summarized version of the text which is dictated by members of the group in turn.

4 When this summary is complete, intervene to discuss errors, and improve on the version if necessary.

5 Ask each individual to make notes from the summary.

6 Send one student with the summary to the other group. (Check when your groups are ready and exchange simultaneously: the first five stages should take approximately thirty minutes.)

7 Ask the visiting student to read out his or her group's summary to the new group, and ask the group to take notes.

8 On completion of the task in step 7 ask the visiting student to return to his or her own group.

9 When the student returns from the other group, his or her own group should tell him or her about the other group's topic.

10 Each group now writes questions to test the comprehension of the other group, who have only *heard* about the text and not *read* it. You should only intervene to correct question forms.

11 You and your colleague then exchange sets of questions and use the questions for discussion purposes.

12 Finally the groups come together to discuss and solve problems arising from the questions, clear up misunderstandings, and express opinions on the texts, etc.

COMMENTS

This activity relies on a co-operative effort with a relatively low teacher profile throughout. It encourages involvement on the part of all the students and it involves all the skills. Depending on the degree of difficulty within the text, e.g. new lexis, embedded sentences, etc., there is an enormous amount of mileage in the activity.

6 Tourist broadsheets

LEVEL

Intermediate to Advanced

AGE

Adolescent upwards

PREPARATION

If you are working in the UK these broadsheets can be produced for other foreign students; if you are working outside the UK, then the broadsheets can be produced for English-speaking tourists or visitors.

PROCEDURE

1 Bring to the class some tourist information brochures, leaflets, handouts, etc., for the students to look at in pairs or groups. Ask your students' opinions of this material, for example:
– *Is anything missing from this information?*
– *Is there anything else we could tell a visitor?*
– *What else goes on that might interest a visitor?*
Ask your students to make suggestions, for example, local customs, folklore, new or future developments in the city, Rag week, favourite student haunts, best restaurants or coffee bars, speciality shops, etc.

2 Discuss with your students how the items to be researched should be allocated.

3 This stage and its management will depend on the items the class suggests; in some cases the students may need to visit somewhere outside the classroom to check on information, maps may need to be drawn, photographs taken, sketches made, reference books used, and notes made. It may be necessary for some students to make phone calls or to consult authoritative sources to verify facts, and you will have to assess how much time to allow for all these things and whether you want them to take up lesson time, or homework time, or both.

4 When all the information has been collected it is useful to set up a workshop session to give everyone the chance to see all the information, and to assess what kind of end product would be appropriate. There are various ways of treating the material:
– one large classroom broadsheet
– single A4 size broadsheets written up by small groups and concentrating on a particular theme, e.g. shops
– if you have access to reproduction facilities, a number of copies run off a single top copy
– small booklets produced in pairs depending on the materials available.
It is not necessary for a unanimous decision to be reached over how to present the information, and provided everyone is involved, the production side can be fairly open-ended as the intention is to use language, not create glossy brochures.

COMMENTS	This activity works well if the students have a specific audience in mind. If your school takes part in an exchange programme, or if certain students are involved in individual exchanges, this is an ideal target. In some towns it is worth approaching the local tourist information office, and asking them to display some of the work, or asking a hotel to make a copy available in the foyer or reception area. You may, however, just wish to keep it within the school, although it is still worth putting the end product on display.

7 Newspaper front page

LEVEL	**All levels**
AGE	**Adolescent upwards** (possibly advanced juniors)
PROCEDURE	**1** Bring to the class several large sheets of card, e.g. 50 cm × 30 cm. You will also need the following: glue, scissors, advertisements, news features, articles, weather reports, photographs, etc., and felt pens.

2 Produce a typewritten handout for the group. This is an example:

Objective: to redesign the front page of a newspaper called the <u>Evening Star</u>.

Time: you have to complete the new design by the end of the lesson, e.g. 1 hour.

In your groups: choose a Manager to decide the overall organization; an Editor to supervise the writing of articles; Journalists to rewrite the articles; an Art Editor to paste up and arrange the items.

Organization: you will receive old articles, advertisements, photographs, etc. from a previous edition of the <u>Evening Star</u>. The management do not like the existing format of the front page so you have been asked to redesign it. You <u>cannot</u> use the articles as they are: you must rewrite them. From time to time you will receive new items and you must decide whether or not to incorporate them into the front page. You may not change the themes, but you can lengthen or shorten the articles. Remember to use headlines, titles, journalists' names. You can use up to six adverts – either unchanged or written by you.

You must fill the blank piece of card.

3 Divide the class into groups (ideally 5 or 6 students in each group), and brief the Managers from each group. The classroom furniture will need rearranging, so that the groups can work around their front page.

4 Periodically you feed in new articles, etc., up to a point about twenty minutes before the end of the lesson.

5 You should circulate but try not to intervene.

6 When the redesigned newspaper front pages are finished, they can be displayed on the wall.

COMMENTS

This is a modified activity from *Simulations in Language Teaching* by Ken Jones and it employs all four skills. The end product is quickly achieved. It encourages imaginative use of language, and is enjoyable to carry out.

2 Organizing a project

What kind of project?

Once you have decided to embark on a fully integrated project you will have to consider the length, scope, and level, but the main question will be, *What kind of project?* The answer to this question will be determined by what interests the students, and how they as a group respond to an idea.

The next important question is, *Where does the initial stimulus come from?* The answer to this question is threefold; it may lie with you, the teacher, it may come from an individual within the group, or it may arise out of the group dynamics with no one clear contributing source. In the first case, a teacher who has a close working relationship with a group and is sensitive to the needs of the group will naturally come to learn about the group's interests. Over a period of time topics will be discussed and some areas of mutual interest will take hold of the imagination more than others. It is these moments of imaginative participation between teacher and students that only you, the teacher, can recognize, and which create an opportunity for exploring an issue in more depth, with a view to the language work arising out of this exploration. The same procedure operates if the idea has come from one individual within the group, or if you are aware that there is suddenly an idea, regardless of how it appeared; it is not important who made the suggestion, it is important that you should recognize it and capitalize on it as the focal point for an extended language activity: *a project.*

There is no shortage of areas of interest from a student's point of view. In one group at an intermediate level, I have come across students concerned with local issues such as conservation, the closure of a school and hospital, and the infrequency of local bus services. On a global scale they have been interested in the long-term effects of acid rain, racial conflict, and space research. In another group at a different level, they have asked what English people do in their spare time, where they like to go for their holidays, and whether it is true that the English care more for their animals than their children! The point I am making, however, is not the all-embracing grandeur of a theme, but whether the subject has potential in terms of a project.

The jumping-off point, then, is the conviction that the subject is worth pursuing, and that there is a strong, corporate desire to pursue it.

Planning a project: the initial stages

As already mentioned, you have to be alert to the possibility of a project, but at the same time you may envisage implementing a project at a particular stage in the course, and therefore need to plan ahead rather than wait for divine inspiration to strike the group. In this case you have to take the initiative, to remain flexible to the group's response to the idea, and to carry out some of the pre-project planning behind the scenes. A long-term project which aims to make a video film, or produce a booklet, wall display, or other tangible end product as part of the language development, will require more detailed planning than the short-term project which depends on getting information from passers-by in the street or tourists arriving at a mainline railway station.

The length of time you spend on a project will vary depending on your own particular circumstances. You may want to concentrate on a project for all the English language lessons during a limited period of two or three weeks. You may see a project as only part of the overall programme, occupying one day a week—there is no hard and fast rule. If you are working outside the UK you will have to consider whether you are likely to need information from the UK, and allow enough time to order this material in advance. It is not, however, necessary to do this, but you must decide how much background material is likely to be needed if the initial impetus is going to be teacher-centred. A lot will depend on how well you know the group and how far you feel the idea can be sustained while the students actually collect the data as part of the project work itself. In one project (described in detail in Chapter 5) my students undertook work in a hospital and spastic unit. This project was deliberately teacher inspired and I had spent a number of hours familiarizing myself with the subject of spasticity, visiting the hospital and the staff concerned, and writing to relevant agencies for information. If the group had ultimately turned down the idea, I would not have felt that my time had been wasted as another group might have responded positively to the same topic at a later date.

Data collection and storage

When data is collected and research carried out, you have to devise a system for storing this information and retrieving it at a later point. It should be borne in mind that researchers will almost certainly not be retrieving their own material, but that others in the group will have to. So the system has to be well organized, easily accessible, clearly indexed, and hard-wearing. A simple cardboard box, or better still, a wooden crate of the type that holds fruit or vegetables, can be cut down to display the materials. A bold card index can be attached to the front. Some materials lend themselves to wall displays, and these can be pinned up for everyone to read.

The system need not be elaborate, but the materials must look attractive and be pitched at the appropriate language level, especially if they are selected by the teacher as opposed to the students. Some materials may need adapting or editing, so that students are not overwhelmed by too much unknown language. Where data collection forms part of the actual project, however, these problems will not arise, as the selection criteria will be imposed by the students themselves. In these circumstances valuable written activities can be set up, for example, based on the need to write to various agencies. (See Chapter 4 for examples.) The materials have to be available to all the students all the time, so some kind of loan scheme needs to be organized by the students themselves if the materials are going to be taken home.

Before your students are sent out collecting information, you should also ensure that they are going to be able to gain access to the various libraries, museums, offices, etc., unless it is envisaged that gaining access is going to be part of a language task. A brief letter or telephone enquiry is usually polite and alerts organizations to the prospect of a student invasion. Even if the students only need to stand in a station forecourt and ask questions of passing travellers, it is best to contact the appropriate authorities beforehand to avoid unforeseen difficulties. In some instances, of course, permission will be refused, and it is worth compiling a list of negative areas for your own use and that of your colleagues. I have also found it a good idea to issue students with bona fides in the form of a small card signed by the school head or principal, which the student can present if challenged over identity or status. (See Figure 2.1 for a suggested format.)

```
Guy Heinkel

is a student at (name of school), (name of

city). If you have any queries please telephone

the school on (telephone number)
                                        Photo
                                        (optional)
Signed:

Principal
```

Figure 2.1

Outside visits and speakers

The question of outside visits and visitors needs careful consideration. Are they always necessary to a project? Certainly the initial stage of a project may benefit from a visit to a relevant organization, or an outsider coming in to talk to the students, but whether this is feasible will depend on your own circumstances. The impetus for a visit may come from the students, and an advanced group may be able to follow up the idea by investigating the possibility for themselves. An outsider, maybe in an official capacity, could contribute to the project by being invited to spend a few hours with the group in the classroom. At the beginning of the *Good wheelchair guide* project (see Chapter 5) the group visited a person confined to a wheelchair in his own home, in this case an acquaintance of mine. As a result of this, the students invited him along to the school and organized his visit themselves. On my instigation, at the start of the *Hospital and spastic unit* project (see Chapter 5) a person suffering from spasticity spent a morning with the group, talking very frankly about his handicap. Another group, who wanted to produce a radio programme, spent a couple of hours at a very tolerant local radio station. In some cases these arrangements have to be made well in advance, particularly visits to busy organizations; the teacher will have to weigh up the potential problem of lining up a visit and of the students ultimately not being interested. Cancelling arrangements at the last minute sets a poor precedent for further requests and could be embarrassing for other colleagues. One way of rescuing the situation is to offer the opportunity to another class. Or the visit could be treated as a one-off without the group knowing that it had been intended as one piece of a long-term jigsaw. This situation is only going to arise, however, when the start of a project is teacher-centred.

Dealing with individual visits from people who may be personal contacts is slightly easier. In these cases I have always taken the individuals into my confidence and warned them that, if the idea does not develop, the need for their services (whether from me or my students) may not materialize. I have yet to come across a group of students who turn down, out of hand, an opportunity to extend their experience. Where requests for visits and contacts are wholly student-centred, it is necessary to rely on an extensive resources list, so that the students can follow up their suggestions as quickly as possible, and this is where your own resources index is so valuable (see Appendix I for a personal resources index).

Materials and equipment

However modest the project, it will undoubtedly incur additional expense. The nature of the project will dictate the kind of equipment, but it is worth investing in some basic materials which can be recycled, such as clipboards, if the school can afford it. It is better not to buy material which is specific to one subject, such as medical textbooks, but to concentrate on items that could be useful for a variety of purposes.

As students will often be working outside the classroom and will need to record information, it is important to have materials available which make this job as easy as possible, for example:
- *Strong clipboards* with an attachment for pen or pencil are invaluable and can be used again and again.
- *Spiral notepads* with stiff covers are a good substitute if clipboards are too expensive, but they are not re-usable.
- *Files* with a combination of plain paper for drawing and lined paper for notes are good for easy insertion or withdrawal of information.
- *Miscellaneous equipment* including coloured pens or felt tips, Blu-Tack, sellotape, glue, coloured card, drawing pins, cork boards for extra classroom display purposes, are all invaluable if it is possible to afford them.
- *Small cassette players* which can be hand held with either an internal or external microphone are ideal for *vox pop.* recordings, i.e. recordings made, often in the street, of people expressing opinions and ideas spontaneously when interviewed.
- *Polaroid cameras* for instant stills which can later be incorporated into personal records or used for broadsheet illustration purposes, are a reasonably cheap source of visual material once the initial outlay has been made on the camera.
- A *video camera and recorder* with playback facilities obviously provide more scope for a school investing in project work. In the early stages of developing project work, however, too much technological hardware may merely get in the way, and back-up technical assistance is usually essential.

It is worth remembering that students may have their own hardware—cameras or cassette recorders, for example—which they will be happy to use for the project, especially if the school does not have any such facilities.

A project will incur expense, but the possibility of hidden costs must not be forgotten. Particularly during a long-term project there will be expenditure which cannot always be foreseen, such as bus fares, if students are travelling beyond walking distance, unpredictable telephone calls, extra polaroid film or flash. Other examples are, a small gift after a visit to an institution or an individual; postage, magazines, tickets for a film which may have a bearing on the group's work, and so on. If you are outside the UK, postage costs may be very high and therefore may be a major item. Some of these extra costs, although cheap in themselves, can mount up, and students may feel resentful if they are expected to contribute out of their own pockets. It is better to alert the group at the start of a project to the possibility of additional expenditure; it is useful to fix a ceiling on the individual contribution, say 50p or £1 each. (Teachers outside the UK will think of a suitable local equivalent.) The easiest way of coping with finances is, if possible, for the school to allocate a fixed sum of petty cash over the length of the project, so that everyone works within this budget.

One major consideration when organizing project work is *where* in the school the project should be based. This decision really has to be taken without reference to the students. A classroom with easy outside access is preferable to one in the heart of the building, especially if there is a lot of coming and going, which could disturb other classes. It is an advantage if the room can be adapted for entertaining visitors, showing films or slides, even wheeling in wheelchairs. Ideally the classroom furniture should be mobile, so that it can be stacked away and reassembled for workshop purposes. Lighting is important, particularly if a video camera is to be used, and blackout facilities are necessary to show a film on a screen. Internal noise can disturb visiting speakers, and noisy discussions, etc., can disturb everyone else. Secure storage facilities are necessary for both the hardware and all the other materials which tend to accumulate.

Checklist
Storage facilities
Display boards
Advance warnings to organizations
Available bona fides
Arrangements for visits and visitors
Extra materials
Financial budget
Project room

Student grouping

Another arrangement which needs sorting out is whether, outside the classroom, students work alone, in pairs or in groups. Before the students leave the classroom it is advisable to discuss with them what arrangements are the most appropriate and allow them to decide. Students working in the UK will run various risks as soon as they leave the school, and unless they are very confident, they are unlikely to want to work alone. You should never underestimate the very real fears of some students that they will actually get lost, or find themselves in socially embarrassing situations. Students working in their own countries run less of a risk in the sense of orientation or encountering socially embarrassing situations, but they will still have

to contend with spontaneous language situations where they need to
manipulate the foreign language with a reasonable degree of skill and
confidence in order to attain their objectives. On the whole pair-work
is more successful than small group-work.

The question of grouping inside the classroom also needs attention.
Certain activities like letter-writing, reporting orally, and keeping a
diary, may begin as group-based activities and develop quite naturally
into individual activities. Other tasks, like creating a wall display,
keeping charts, or making a broadsheet, lend themselves to group-
work. You may want to try pyramid-building techniques, setting
individual assignments for homework, pairing students during class
time, and then re-grouping into larger groups. The point to remember
is that the work can only develop along lines which you and your
students work out together, and therefore the approach must be
flexible; you may have your own ideas as to what you might like to see
developing, but cannot impose these ideas.

The development of the project

To start with the finish—there need not always be a tangible end
product. A group's language needs will differ. Students planning a
holiday in the UK through an exchange programme will have very
different needs from a group of foreign teachers in the UK who are
there to update their own language skills; a group of students going on
to university in the UK may benefit from a project concentrating on
written language, whereas a group of twelve-year-olds on a short trip
will benefit from a project concentrating on spoken and listening skills.
The language objectives may suggest a tangible objective, as did the
investigation into the facilities for wheelchairs, but the end product
needs to be kept in perspective so that it does not dominate the
language development; the end product is merely a vehicle for more
related language work. It is, however, important that the work on the
project comes to an end either because something has been achieved,
or because the students feel it is time for it to come to an end. It should
not just be stopped because you have had enough of it. As to what kind
of end product results from project work, the answer to this question
is, almost anything. Broadsheets, handouts, mock newspapers, radio
programmes, case studies, booklets, wall displays, video programmes,
parties, group reports, diaries. The list could be endless and the final
outcome may be very different from what was initially envisaged. Or,
as has already been said, a tangible end product may never materialize
at all.

Getting a project started

Getting a project off the ground successfully will depend on a number of factors: exposure to the kinds of activities outlined in Chapter 1, the rapport between you and your students, the choice of project topic, and the way in which the group works together. During lessons with the students you will have become familiar with their reactions and motivation in handling communicative activities, and will have learnt whether they find these activities useful, enjoyable, and a successful way of learning new language. If their reactions are positive then the time is right to broach a project. This may take anything from one day to three months. Assuming agreement has been reached that a project sounds like a good idea, what next? If you have access to your own or somebody else's previous project work, and can describe or display what was done, this always acts as a stimulus. If there is no previous project work, then you have to rely on enthusiasm and the ability to inspire a group, and then allow them to field both their own ideas and yours, rather like a brain-storming session. I hope this does not sound vague or ultimately unhelpful; any teacher who has read this far will have realized the open-ended nature of project work and will appreciate that there is no magic formula, except perhaps the phrase, *Why don't we . . . ?* This brain-storming session can be time-consuming and even emotionally exhausting; you may have to respond to a series of *ad hoc* demands and questions only to find that the initial enthusiasm does not continue. It may be disappointing, but on the positive side the experience will no doubt prove useful when the next occasion presents itself.

Once the idea of a project has been accepted, there has to be an 'incubation period' during which time you and your group mull over ideas, perhaps informally exchanging suggestions, etc. Some members of the group may be reluctant to participate and may come up with an alternative suggestion or programme. There may be one or two individuals who genuinely dislike the whole concept of a project, or who don't identify with the group. In these cases ways have to be found to involve people, or else a separate timetable will have to be devised as an alternative to project work. One can usually find a way round these problems because the team spirit in a class is often very strong. I once had a student who was very reluctant to work outside the classroom but her willingness to collate data brought in by the others was invaluable. Moreover, she provided a willing ear when everyone returned and wanted to talk about what had happened outside.

Problems in the early stages

Once the idea has been fully accepted, you need to take the group into your confidence over possible pitfalls and problems, as well as the ways in which they envisage the integration of all the skills, and where they might concentrate on certain skills as opposed to others. You should try to ensure that the students feel that you are exploring the possibilities with them and not ahead of them. By listening to and considering the students' opinions, and making your opinion secondary, you will let them know that each and every contribution they make is important. Individual students should be encouraged to lead discussions and make suggestions over how to structure activities, what needs to be done, and what language skills will be needed to achieve these ends. At the start of the *Good wheelchair guide* project, one of the students volunteered the fact that he had a disabled brother, and that he spent every weekend working with disabled people. In the *Primary school teaching* project (see Chapter 5), one student had worked in youth clubs, and another on holiday adventure programmes, and had an instinct for the sorts of things young children enjoyed doing. In the *Hospital and spastic unit* project, one student had never been inside a hospital in her life; her admission of fear turned out to be a great asset, as it brought out other students' inhibitions, and gave rise to a lot of valuable language work in expressing anxieties and fears. The point is that these reactions cannot be anticipated, but the chances are that the impetus will be maintained and built upon by you and your students.

Finally some words of warning as to what can go wrong at the start of a project. After the initial burst of enthusiasm, there is often a period of anti-climax, when everyone begins to worry about coping with learning the new language which is going to be required for specific situations. Or they suddenly feel overwhelmed by all they want to undertake. This seems a natural reaction, not just the reaction of the EFL classroom: people need reassurance and encouragement to tackle what is new and strange. A new topic area will quickly stimulate the need to acquire new vocabulary, and it is a good idea to have ready a way of coping with this demand. If students feel that new language will neither overwhelm them nor disappear before they can grasp it, they will have conquered one of the things that can turn a project sour. One suggestion is to produce a vocabulary monitor (see Figure 2.2). Every time students come across a new word or phrase, whether inside or outside the classroom, they record it on a piece of card and slip the card into one of the transparent pockets. This allows other students to read it, to add anything they wish, and to absorb the word and the way it is used in its correct context. The vocabulary monitor remains on the wall throughout the project, constantly available for reinforcement and consolidation. It can be altered or added to at any stage, and is a source of vocabulary games. Other problem areas are discussed in Chapters 3 and 4.

Week 1

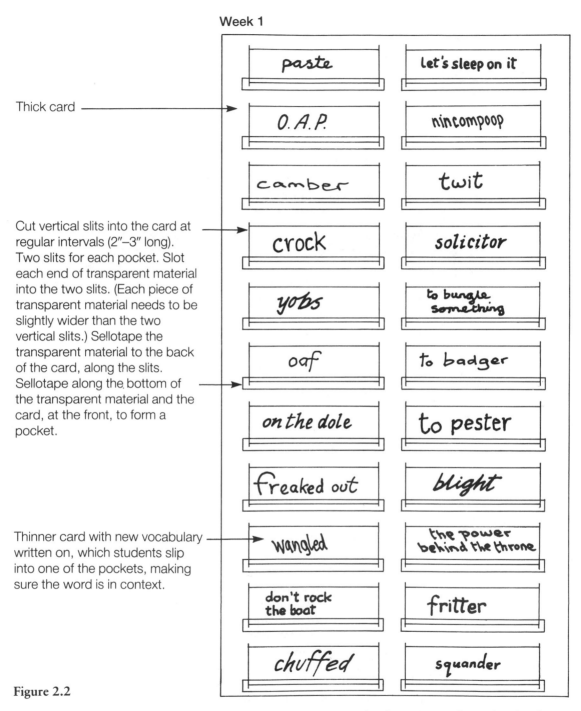

Thick card

Cut vertical slits into the card at regular intervals (2″–3″ long). Two slits for each pocket. Slot each end of transparent material into the two slits. (Each piece of transparent material needs to be slightly wider than the two vertical slits.) Sellotape the transparent material to the back of the card, along the slits. Sellotape along the bottom of the transparent material and the card, at the front, to form a pocket.

Thinner card with new vocabulary written on, which students slip into one of the pockets, making sure the word is in context.

Figure 2.2

One final warning: spontaneous enthusiasm cannot be maintained, especially during long-term projects, and eventually evaporates. With certain groups I have intervened to tone down a project, or suggested a completely different activity, or deliberately staged a teacher-centred, non-project lesson in order to maintain rapport and stability within the group.

3 The project in action

Role of the teacher

Whatever the scope of a project, whatever the language level, and whether you are teaching in the UK or overseas, your role as a teacher involved in project work remains fundamentally the same: a participant, a co-ordinator when necessary, a figure in the background evaluating and monitoring the language being used.

According to Littlewood (*Communicative Language Teaching*, 1981) 'the students' range of communicative needs is limited by the nature of the classroom'. While this holds true for activities based solely within the classroom, one of the objects of project work is that it should operate for some of the time outside the classroom. This makes your role within the classroom even more vital, because there is a need to gain maximum benefit from the classroom sessions, interspersed as they may be with outside work. You will need to develop strategies (see *Monitoring* on page 39) for handling the language which has arisen from learner-centred activities in an authentic but unpredictable environment outside the classroom.

Short-term projects

Since shortage of time can limit the number of language activities, it is necessary to define the sequence of tasks clearly to maximize the time available for active use of the language.

If intermediate level students are going to spend an hour, which is a long time, operating in a high-risk situation (e.g. interviewing passengers in a station concourse), then the language input will have to focus on the structures used for polite intervention and withdrawal needed for this purpose. Students will also have to tackle the area of questionnaire design (depending on what they are hoping to find out through the interviews) in order to record written information. Other language will obviously arise at random, but if the sole objective has been to conduct successful interviews, in order to elicit specific information, then the monitoring of the language remains straightforward. Back in the classroom, other language activities may derive from the original idea, and these related communicative skills are discussed in Chapter 4.

Long-term projects

The long-term project has so many ramifications that at its outset it is impossible to perceive an overall structuring of the language content. As the project develops and the students respond and innovate, you will find yourself responding and innovating. A forward planning process to systematize the language input is difficult, though where students request specific language some of the teaching can be developed along more structured lines. A weekly review of what has actually been generated in active language usage is a helpful means of ensuring that the language work does not become too haphazard. The development of the four skills with systematic checklists is discussed in Chapter 4. The weekly review (see Figure 3.1) is designed to be completed by the students. You will also have your own weekly teaching scheme, which will be partly forward planning as you anticipate student language needs, and partly retrospective completion as you review what has actually happened. It is useful to collect in the group's reviews and to compare them with your summary as well as with each other. It is advisable to return these at the start of the next week, and indicate omissions or other points relevant to the individual's work. This is time-consuming but is of enormous benefit to both you and your students.

Another important factor associated with the long-term project is that your role may seem to be weakened at times, particularly in the eyes of your colleagues. It may seem as if you are not actually doing anything, in the sense of preparing conventional lesson plans, for example. The irony is of course that the more passive you appear to be, the more successful the project. Nevertheless, it would be totally misleading to suggest that passivity reflects inactivity. The sensitive teacher provides moral support in such a way that the students hardly notice you. Simply *being* with the group, working along with them, awaiting their return, if they are undertaking something alone, and being absorbed in how they are handling their own language needs, enables you to hold the group together without overtly and busily *doing* anything.

Monitoring

Though I have argued for a role of non-intervention for part of the time that the teacher and group are working on a project, it is necessary to devise strategies for monitoring what is going on in terms of language usage. You, the teacher, need to know whether your students are actually learning anything, and they need to know whether they are making progress, and what particular aspects of their own work needs improvement. Your role in monitoring these factors is crucial.

Weekly review

Name ....

Class ....

Dates ....

1 What new vocabulary have you learnt this week?
....
....

2 Which of these new words can you use with confidence?
....
....

3 Which of these new words do you feel unsure about?
....
....

4 What can you say/do this week that you couldn't say/do last week?
....
....

5 What have you learnt about the language that you didn't know before this week?
....
....

6 What have you read this week? ....
    What have you listened to this week? ....
    What have you written about this week? ....
    What have you spoken about this week? ....
7 Did you use any textbooks this week?
....
....

8 What homework have you done this week?
....
....

9 Any comments?
....
....

Figure 3.1

You may make photocopies of this page for classroom use (but please note that copyright law does not normally permit multiple copying of published material).

The short-term project, in which a group of students collect their data in a matter of a few hours, either conducting street interviews, visiting a local factory, or conducting a census of the number of tourists leaving the railway station, provides a fairly clearly defined framework for monitoring the language.

To give an example, you may be solely concerned with the students' ability to interrupt appropriately, e.g. 'Excuse me, I wonder if you would mind answering a few questions, please', (in formal situations) as opposed to 'Please, I want you to answer my questions', or 'Pardon, will you answer my questions?', etc. If you circulate freely and concentrate on this particular structure or function, it is easy enough to make discreet notes of errors at random—either grammatical or phonological, and ascribe specific errors to specific students. From the actual monitoring point of view there will be a good deal of redundant language. Some of it may be significant and suggest further practice at a later stage, so that making a note of these items is very worthwhile, particularly if they are dealt with quickly while still fresh in the students' minds.

On certain occasions while circulating among the groups, you can carry out discreet checks on the language being used by means of error analysis sheets; these sheets can be designed to suit the level of the students and the target language (see Figures 3.2 and 3.3).

Figure 3.2 is a fairly open-ended method for monitoring error, but can be unwieldy if one is dealing with too many students at once, as each student requires a separate sheet. Devise your own system of symbols for error analysis, and encourage your students to practise self-correction. You can record what you consider to be the most serious errors in the left-hand column, using a symbol to indicate the kind of error. Then the student can write in the correction in the right-hand column. This method is greatly appreciated by all students, whatever their level. When they realize that their efforts to practise and sustain language are not going unheeded, the students gain confidence in the teacher, which is essential to project work.

Figure 3.3 shows an error monitor sheet which attempts to categorize the errors students are likely to make. This is useful when it comes to seeing a pattern in student-error frequency, but can slow down the actual recording process if you have to stop and categorize the error in the first place. Again these sheets can be individualized, and over a long-term project the personal record is invaluable, particularly when students can look back to see the mistakes made in the past which they don't make any more.

Students at upper intermediate or advanced levels can be encouraged to monitor each other using the error monitor sheets, but this kind of decision will depend on the rapport within the group. It may work for certain nationalities, but other nationalities will be reluctant or resentful if they know that their peers are recording their mistakes, or else feel that what they consider to be the teacher's role is being usurped.

ERROR MONITOR

Name: ....   Week 1/Monday 2 4 Nov.

Error	Correction
What means this? Q	What does this mean?

Quick-reference symbols:

L - lexis	str. - structure
pron. - pronunciation	w.o. - word order
T - tense	Q - question form

Figure 3.2

You may make photocopies of this page for classroom use (but please note that copyright law does not normally permit multiple copying of published material).

Monitoring does not always mean systematic recording of one kind or another; if students are scattered around a town, or outside in pairs or small groups, you can look in on groups if you have access to transport, so long as your presence is not disruptive. During the *Hospital and spastic unit* project it was enough for me to make quick visits to the various wards to ensure all was well; in most cases the individual students didn't even notice me, but they knew that periodically I would appear, and if they needed me I was available. At this level I relied very much on the students' ability to monitor for themselves, and allowed time for extensive feedback sessions to listen, read, and talk about what they had been doing.

ERROR MONITOR

Name: ....

Grammatical	Phonological	Functional/ Appropriacy	Other e.g. Lexis
What *means X*? May I have a bread, please?	I/*ka:nt*/swim hospital	(for advice) you must stay at home (on telephone) I am Hans.	I am hangover. When babies start to crumble...

Figure 3.3

You may make photocopies of this page for classroom use (but please note that copyright law does not normally permit multiple copying of published material).

The use of audio or video monitoring equipment adds another dimension to the monitoring, in that activities can be replayed, and if necessary previewed prior to exploitation in the classroom, but such equipment is not available to many teachers at present. Besides, the presence of such equipment can inhibit students, apart from any problems of transportation. If available, video or tape-recordings can become a part of the project—they could be the end product. In that case, the recordings might well provide material for analysis.

Classroom feedback sessions

If you and your students are going to exploit the recorded language data during group sessions in the classroom, then you must ensure that you focus on what is significant and useful for everyone, and avoid laborious verbatim sessions, which can be boring and time-consuming. It is also important to encourage contributions from everyone, not the best raconteurs.

If the project is moving very quickly, a lot of half-learnt, half-understood language items may begin to accumulate. Specific homework tasks can be set, in which students are encouraged to log some of these items for presentation in class. These items can then be used as a springboard for more intensive work, and during a long-term project a dossier can be built up for both diagnostic and remedial purposes. With an advanced level group try giving out these items among the group and asking them to prepare micro-teaching slots, in which they teach the rest of the group. Items can range from specific grammatical points to functions, idioms, phonological points, and even factual information on some aspect of English history.

Some feedback sessions may turn into a workshop; students may be sorting out their materials, making wall displays, writing up reports, preparing or designing questionnaires, etc., and your role is one of constant participation, even though you yourself may not be in charge of anything specific.

If students have recorded an interview, this will also require looking at, but it is not necessary for everyone to read, listen, and talk about everything. Encourage your students to be selective; get them to pick out the best bits of a recording, and just listen to those particular bits. Sometimes you can vary the techniques during the feedback: make everything available on a deliberately random basis, and leave the students to pursue what interests them. This can also be quite revealing from your point of view. At one stage during a long-term project we were inundated with audio recordings, notes from the interviews, maps, printed handouts which the students had been given, and photographs. We pushed all the desks together, piled everything in the centre, and for a while everyone circulated freely until it appeared that everyone wanted to read the notes from the interviews.

At some stage during a project you may discover films, radio programmes, newspaper articles, or other published material which has a bearing on what your group is doing. It may not be feasible for everyone to keep up to date all the time with fresh material. Ask for volunteers to watch a particular programme or read an article, and then set aside class time for the rest of the group to be told about what they have missed. Students can be encouraged to watch out for these relevant items themselves, but it is up to you to exploit this interest and to provide time for people to share their experiences. Even the more reluctant members of a group are often drawn into this useful activity, and go off to read and watch things which they would have been unlikely to do on their own initiative.

You also need to be sensitive to the relationships within the group, and over the course of a long-term project you will probably find that some feedback sessions become discussions of students' relationships with each other or with you. Provided these discussions are constructive and without acrimony, they are useful pointers to what is working well and what may need to be put on one side because it causes difficulties of one kind or another.

Dealing with difficulties

However well a project appears to be progressing, there will always be occasions when things go wrong. I have never tackled a long-term project when there have not been problems: relationships may sour, certain students drop out of the group commitment, or others become downright uncooperative. None of these problems has meant that the project has folded, so you should not panic or imagine that the problems are insurmountable. In the first instance, if there are personality problems, try to allow time for the group to sort them out. If the group runs into serious difficulties, then you may need to intervene for an open discussion of what has gone wrong and what can be done about it. Project work involves a sense of commitment which is not a part of more conventional teaching, and many students may not at first realize how strong their commitment is and how much they personally have invested in their work. This is only likely to arise during a long-term project, but it is worth discussing with your students if you feel it may be at the root of the problem.

Sometimes a day off or a day spent doing something different or going out together is all that is needed. Another possibility is to have a series of lessons which make no reference to the project. Again, during a long-term project, lack of confidence or boredom can occur, or the language learning may seem to have reached a plateau. Interim progress reports can be used to help ease the situation: other staff and students can be invited along to listen to what the group is doing, and, if appropriate, to pass comments, give advice, or make suggestions. This usually works well, and fosters a sense of achievement, as well as acting as a spur. If things are going very badly, however, you can wind up the project work on as positive a note as possible, detailing all the items that had been learnt through doing it, and minimizing the fact that the long-term goal had not been reached.

4 The layered approach

Developing the four skills

In this chapter there is a breakdown of the ways in which the four skills come into operation during the course of a project. In Chapter 3 it was pointed out that at the start of a project it is almost impossible to see how to structure the language content. Nevertheless, if you are to avoid being submerged in a mass of new language, and your students are to see some sequence in what they are learning, there has to be some framework to make this possible. The *layered approach* (Figure 4.1) illustrates how the skills interweave, how certain skills are used more intensively at some stages of a project than at others, and how the skills are wholly interdependent. The layered approach illustrates how skills develop in layers, or cumulatively, the basis for the development being the reading, listening, and speaking skills—not necessarily in any order but dependent on the objectives and the language needs of the group. As already mentioned, different project objectives require different emphases: a review of a city's restaurants will require a different set of skills from those required to produce a short radio programme.

The language level of the group will determine the objective, and although the layered approach remains constant, the range and variety of the skills which develop will always remain as variables. Overall, however, the skills are by definition, integrated, regardless of whether the project is short-term or long-term.

The concept of the layered approach is intended to give an idea of the skills which arise out of project work, and how they extend the kinds of activities described in Chapter 1. No two projects will ever be the same, but there is a progression of skills which is characteristic of all project work. You will need to modify and adapt the model together with your students. The main purpose of the diagram is to indicate the enormous potential of this approach to language learning. The blank model (Figure 4.2) is for your use in order to record your own projects.

'Layered' approach to project work

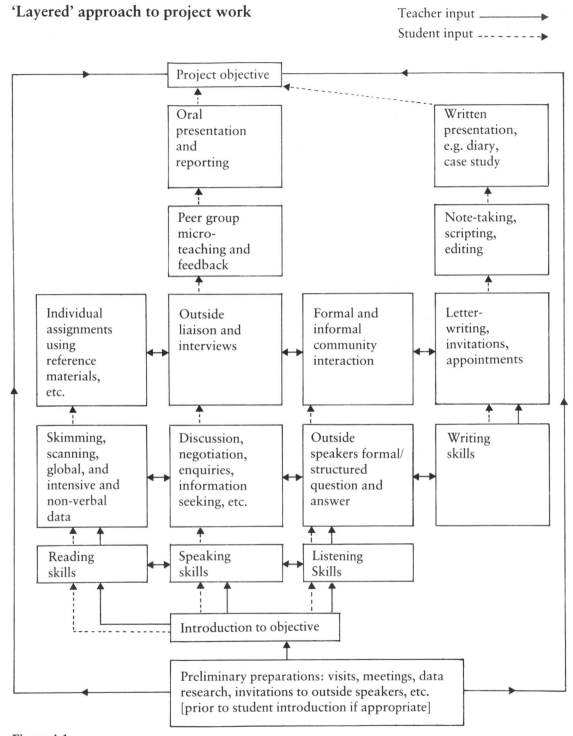

Teacher input ⟶

Student input ⟶

Figure 4.1

'Layered' approach to project work

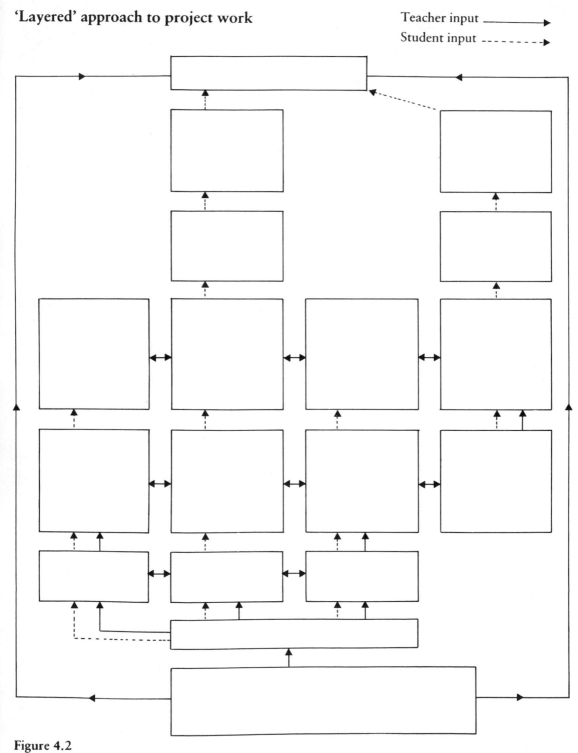

Figure 4.2

You may make photocopies of this page for classroom use (but please note that copyright law does not normally permit multiple copying of published material).

One of the perennial difficulties you have to face before a project develops is to try and anticipate the sub-skills which are likely to occur during a project. The student-centred direction of a project means that you cannot approach a project with any prescribed list of sub-skills. What you can do, however, is to build up checklists of the potential sub-skills (Figures 4.3, 4.4, 4.5, and 4.6 are examples of sub-skills checklists) in order to see their interrelationships. These checklists can then be used to meet student language needs. The checklists also help, even if only in retrospect, to show a coherent overall design to the project and their related language development.

SUB-SKILLS CHECKLIST

Project with class: .... Dates: ....

Speaking	Listening	Reading	Writing
initiating stating agreeing disagreeing interrupting apologizing	gist global	inferencing sequencing skimming scanning reference non-verbal data	note-taking formal letters informal letters instructions

Figure 4.3

SPEAKING AND LISTENING

Skills/activities	Significance within project
short role play extended role play simulation off-air video visits (teacher centred) outside speakers pyramid discussion conflict cue cards language laboratory	street interviews one-to-one encounters building up confidence for 'high risk' situations highlighting specific language practice dialogue/colloquial forms experience for coping 'alone' recognition of discourse features, body language coping with spontaneous language practice encountering hostility practice for interrogative

Figure 4.4

READING SKILLS

Skills	Significance within project
intensive global reference non-verbal data	briefing materials briefing materials dictionaries, encyclopaedia, directories timetables, statistics, maps

Figure 4.5

WRITING SKILLS

Skills	Project related activity
note-taking	recording information from interviews and fieldwork
formal/informal letters	requests for visits, speakers, information enquiries invitations 'thank you' 'bread and butter'
labelling	visual/wall displays
direct v. indirect speech	video scripting radio scripting questionnaire design
appreciation of/reproduction of typeface	presentation and format for end product

Figure 4.6

In addition to these sub-skills checklists, it is also possible to build up and catalogue the language structures and functions, in order to have a readily accessible reference system for teacher-centred lessons which need to focus on specific language items (see Figure 4.7).

The last part of this chapter is an illustration of how this approach is applied, the *Seed project*. This details the organization, procedure, layered approach, and sub-skills checklists, together with a student observation record card (see Figures 4.8, 4.9 and 4.10).

CHECKLIST FOR PROJECT WORK WITH INTERMEDIATE-ADVANCED LEVELS

Structure	Function	Support material
I wonder/was wondering if/whether it is convenient/ it would be convenient for you . . .	initiating for street interviews	role play cue cards simulation e.g. *A Case for English* (CUP, Poté, Hicks et al)
Would you mind answering a few questions? Excuse me...	interruption device	role play

Figure 4.7

Language skills—layered approach

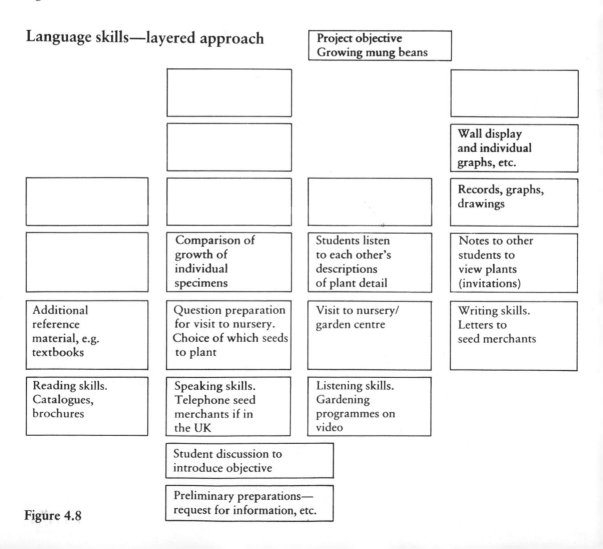

Project objective
Growing mung beans

Wall display and individual graphs, etc.

Records, graphs, drawings

Comparison of growth of individual specimens

Students listen to each other's descriptions of plant detail

Notes to other students to view plants (invitations)

Additional reference material, e.g. textbooks

Question preparation for visit to nursery. Choice of which seeds to plant

Visit to nursery/ garden centre

Writing skills. Letters to seed merchants

Reading skills. Catalogues, brochures

Speaking skills. Telephone seed merchants if in the UK

Listening skills. Gardening programmes on video

Student discussion to introduce objective

Preliminary preparations— request for information, etc.

Figure 4.8

SUB-SKILLS CHECKLIST

Project with class 2: Plant growing   **Dates:** ....

Speaking	Listening	Reading	Writing
initiating stating agreeing disagreeing requesting info. asking formal qs. asking informal qs. thanking introduction	gist global	inferencing skimming scanning reference non-verbal data sequencing matching	note-taking formal letters instructions informal letters non-verbal records

Structure	Function	Support material
imperatives e.g. water daily, keep away from direct sunlight My plant's (bigger than/ smaller than) yours	instruction comparison	game e.g. 'Simon says' origami—making a paper model as a class activity different size bricks, etc. for quick drill around a model structure

Speaking skills	Listening skills	Reading skills	Writing skills
somebody introduce themselves at nursery informal question and answer session	exposure to non- standard accents in UK	seed catalogues textbook references subject specific dependent on student level	keeping a chart/ record of plant growth both verbal/ non-verbal graphs block diagrams drawing and labelling

Figure 4.9

STUDENT OBSERVATION RECORD

Name .... Date .... Class ....

Name of plant   ....

Date planted   ....

Special instructions   ....

Special observations   ....

Graph showing growth rate

Height

Dates

Drawings

1 week	2 weeks	3 weeks	Fully grown

Figure 4.10

You may make photocopies of this page for classroom use (but please note that copyright law does not normally permit multiple copying of published material).

8 Seed project

LEVEL   Intermediate

AGE   Junior to Adolescent

PROCEDURE   1 Tell your students that the topics to be discussed are plants, crops, and food. Ask your students questions such as, e.g.
— *Have you ever seen* (mung beans)?
— *Have you ever eaten* (mung beans)?
— *Have you ever seen* (mung beans) *growing?*

2 If possible, show your students either pictures or photographs of the mung beans or whatever plant is used. Encourage your students to ask questions about growing seeds or plants to elicit:
— *Why don't we grow* (mung beans) *in the classroom?*
Otherwise you make the suggestion yourself.

3 You can either bring to the class some seed catalogues or brochures, or alternatively you can ask your students to write to seed manufacturers themselves.

4 A visit to a nursery or garden centre to see the actual product while waiting for the brochures, would sustain your students' interest.

5 Once the seeds have been ordered and have arrived, your students can choose their variety.

6 Either you or your students can obtain the pots and compost, which can be bought, or borrowed from home. If your students are young, they can be encouraged to write a note to their parents in English (which they can translate orally if necessary) saying why they need the materials.

7 Finally decide, with the students, how the project should procede, whether as a group, in pairs, or individually.

From now on the use made of the project objective as a language activator will be determined by you or your students, to correspond with the growth of the plants, and the language required to express and record the development of the plants.

5 Case studies

Full-scale projects

This chapter describes seven projects which have all been tried by the author and have proved to be successful. These case studies are intended as a source of inspiration for those teachers aiming to incorporate project work into their teaching. They should *not* be followed exactly—that would deny the very principles on which project work rests. The case studies are itemized in a series of sub-headings. These sub-headings (described below) are for teachers to use as an initial aid to breaking down a project into its component parts, so it is clear what has to be done and when, in terms of both language and the project itself.

Level and Age
Intermediate, upper intermediate, advanced, and all levels. Suggested lower age is given.

Time
Anticipated time to be spent, anything from three hours to twelve weeks.

Objectives
Describes the various aims of a project, the skills involved, the tangible end product (if appropriate), the social and personal gains.

Location
Where the project can operate—in the UK, outside the UK, or both, and whether suitable for town, country, etc.

Equipment
Materials needed over and above normal classroom materials (see Chapter 2 for details).

Teacher preparation
Consideration of language input: structure/function/lexis; need for role play/simulation; areas envisaged for operating, e.g. outside a railway station; liaison with outside speakers, other agencies; collecting background information; anticipating problems, e.g. costs, transport, etc.

Student preparation
Ranges from nothing to be done, to pre-project orientation, e.g. visits, background reading, collecting data, listening to programmes, watching videos, classroom discussion.

Organization
Dependent on the length and nature of the project, but mainly covers the logistics outside the classroom.

Skills
Anticipating skills involved: refer to the layered approach and sub-skills checklists in Chapter 4 to determine which skills are likely to operate.

Follow-up
Consideration of how to exploit and develop the work will vary from project to project and from being pre-determined to *ad hoc*.

The case studies
Expedition task
Street interviews
String and pin display
Third world display
Good wheelchair guide
Primary school teaching
Hospital/Spastic unit

Project checklist
Level
Age
Time
Objectives
Location
Equipment
Teacher preparation
Student preparation
Organization
Skills
Follow-up

9 Expedition task for the start of a course

LEVEL	**Intermediate to Advanced**
AGE	**Young adolescent upwards**
TIME	**Three hours** (preferably 15 minutes + 45 minutes, followed by two hours, ideally, but not necessarily, within one working day).
OBJECTIVES	To involve your students in the community; to expose them to authentic language and foreign culture (UK only); to encourage note-taking.
LOCATION	UK or English-speaking enclave, small town to large city.
EQUIPMENT	Pencils, notebooks, transport to city centre or appropriate catchment area, street maps if necessary; card or board for wall display; polaroid camera (optional).

TEACHER PREPARATION

1 Make a list of questions appropriate to your students' language level, although this exercise can be pitched higher without fear of jeopardizing the task.

2 The following are suggested areas for questions, although you will obviously draw on your own knowledge of the local conditions:
– public holidays
– theatre/cinema programmes
– specialist shops
– library opening hours
– bus numbers and routes
– personalities in public life
– cost of food, dry-cleaning, newspapers, etc.

3 The meaning of idioms, current slang, acronyms, logos, etc., can also be pursued. The following question types could be used:
– *What's on at the Odeon cinema this week?*
– *When is the next public holiday?*
– *What time does the library open?*
– *What's the name of the Mayor?*

STUDENT PREPARATION

None.

ORGANIZATION

1 You should brief your students in the classroom; they will have approximately 30 minutes to get the answers to their set of questions from passers-by.

2 Each student has a different set of questions, the numbers depending on the difficulty and language level of the group. The students should work in pairs or individually.

3 At the appointed time, whether or not they have finished, they should return to the pre-arranged pick-up point.

SKILLS

1 Interrupting, asking a question, thanking, apologizing, repeating, withdrawing, etc. (An advanced group is unlikely to require any bridging activities; an intermediate group may require bridging activities, depending on their ability.)

2 Direct versus indirect speech.

FOLLOW-UP

In the classroom the students (in their pairs or individually) present their particular set of questions and answers to the rest of the group. The students can record the information on card, etc., for a wall display; the information can be recorded at random, or classified by topic. You should only intervene if it becomes necessary to clarify or explain anything. At the end of the session your students will have produced a permanent information sheet for reference, alteration, up-dating, etc., during the course, illustrated with photographs, if applicable.

10 Street interviews on a specific topic

LEVEL

Intermediate to Advanced

AGE

Adolescent upwards

TIME

6–8 hours (ideally over one week)

OBJECTIVES

To allow your students sustained communicative practice; to involve them in the community; to design a questionnaire; to provide an opportunity for audio or video recording.

LOCATION

UK or English-speaking enclave or area visited by English-speaking tourists, e.g. station or airport concourse, tourist attraction, etc.

EQUIPMENT

Clipboards, pencils, tape-recorder, portable video or polaroid cameras (if available), transport to the interview point.

TEACHER PREPARATION

Language input using role play if necessary; collecting hardware, e.g. clipboards, cassette recorders; investigating suitable site with a large catchment area, bearing in mind the need to avoid bottlenecks; questionnaire design and back-up for your students' preparation.

STUDENT PREPARATION

Classroom discussion to find areas of interest; selection of topic and discussion of appropriate end product; questionnaire design; individual or pair-work to produce questionnaire sheet.

ORGANIZATION

1 Ask your students to prepare the questionnaire in the classroom, with your help. Use simulation or role-play exercises to prepare them for difficult interviewees, if required.

2 The students organize working groups for the real-life street interviews, allocating tasks and ensuring a rotation of jobs.

3 You will need to deliver the students and their equipment to the catchment area and instruct them to scatter. Everyone should return to the pick-up point at a pre-arranged time.

SKILLS

1 Interview techniques; sub-skills—interrupting, repeating, eliciting, probing, concluding, etc.

2 Written skills: question forms and recording written information if audio or video recordings are not being made.

3 Non-UK location: students will need to preface their interviews with a formula, e.g.
– *Excuse me, do you speak English?*

FOLLOW-UP

The students present the results of their interviews to each other in class. Play back the audio or visual material for language and error analysis, etc., if appropriate. Ask your students to prepare a written record of selected interviews. You can set up an editing session of the audio recordings and get the students to produce a listening package which can be presented to another group. Finally, you could have a discussion on body language.

11 String and pin display: tourist destinations within a town

LEVEL	**Intermediate to Advanced**
AGE	**Adolescent upwards**
TIME	**Approximately 8–10 hours over two weeks**

OBJECTIVES

To produce a 'string and pin' display for public information; to increase your students' confidence in handling casual encounters.

LOCATION

Anywhere which can guarantee a reasonable number of tourists, e.g. railway station, coach or bus terminal, airport, ferry terminal, or established tourist attraction, e.g. Eiffel Tower, civic or parliament buildings, museums, etc.

EQUIPMENT

Clipboards; one map per interviewer *or* a diagrammatic representation which locates tourist attractions, *or* a 'top ten' checklist; cork board, wall display facility; cotton or fine string (ideally coloured); pins—preferably with coloured heads to match the cotton; large street map, hand drawn for final display; transport to the interview points.

TEACHER PREPARATION

1 Discuss with your group the tourist attractions within your town or city.

2 Ask the students, in pairs or as a homework task, to list and/or rank these tourist destinations. The list can then be exploited for presentation of non-verbal information, e.g. block graphs/ histograms, etc.

3 Agree with the whole class on the number of interviews required in order to draw conclusions.

STUDENT PREPARATION

They start by listing the tourist destinations. They agree on the approach, i.e. show a tourist a 'top ten' list and ask whether the tourist intends to visit any or all of these. Or show a tourist a map with attractions highlighted and ask the tourist to indicate his or her intentions. The students should then prepare sheets for recording the answers (see Figure 5.1).

Tourist attraction/destination		Numbers
Castle		ⅲⅲⅲ ⅲⅲⅲ ⅲⅲⅲ ⅲⅲⅲ ⅲⅲⅲ 1
Museum		ⅲⅲⅲ 111
Park		ⅲⅲⅲ ⅲⅲⅲ ⅲⅲⅲ 111
Market		ⅲⅲⅲ ⅲⅲⅲ 11
Statue		111
Other (Library, Old city wall)		ⅲⅲⅲ 111

Figure 5.1

ORGANIZATION

1 You will need to transport your students to strategic areas around your town or city.

2 Your students work in pairs in order to conduct the interviews as quickly as possible, e.g. one person to talk and one to record, and then they should change roles. Advanced level students who can conduct the interview fairly smoothly, may also like to ask the interviewee's nationality in order to follow up the correlation between nationality and sightseeing intentions.

3 In class, in small groups, the students collate the data, using the blackboard.

SKILLS

1 Interview techniques: sub-skills (see *Street interviews* on page 58).

2 Various structures depending on the level of your students, for example:
— *Are you going to . . . ?*
— *What do you intend seeing/doing/visiting?*
— *What do you most want to see?*
— *Where are you going first?* etc.

3 Conditional practice, e.g.
– *If you have time, what do you want to see?*

4 Simple past and present perfect usage, e.g. where the tourist has been in the town for a day or more, questions such as the following will need to be used:
– *Did you see . . . ?*
– *Have you been to . . . ?*

FOLLOW-UP

In the classroom ask the students to discuss as a group, how the interviews went, and try to guess the results before they are actually known. Ask them to place the coloured pins and threads from written labels or visuals, on the large wall mounted street map. The histograms and pie charts can be used to accompany the display (see Figure 5.2).

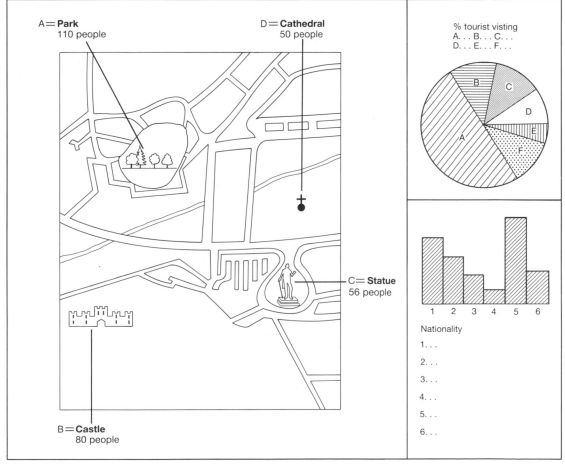

Figure 5.2

We carried out our survey over two weeks and interviewed 200 people. From our survey it shows that A, B, and C are the most popular tourist attractions and that most tourists came from 1 and 5. Further written practice can also be based on the results and can be tackled in a variety of ways from the personal and subjective account of the interview experience, to the formal report.

12 Third world display

LEVEL	**Upper intermediate to Advanced**
AGE	**Young adult upwards**
TIME	**8–10 hours over 2–4 weeks**

OBJECTIVES

To encourage an awareness of issues affecting developing countries and to enable your students to discuss these issues; to produce a wall display; to make posters (see Figure 5.3); to build a shanty house (see Figure 5.4); to organize an austerity lunch or supper: this objective works particularly well if combined with World Food Day (October 16th each year) when students can rely on extra publicity and information from the media in their own country, as well as being able to get information from the Food and Agriculture Organization (FAO) in Rome (see Appendix I for the address), in various languages in addition to English.

LOCATION

Any classroom for initial work. A public thoroughfare in a school, college, street, park, etc., which can guarantee exposure to casual passers-by for the later stages.

EQUIPMENT

Wall or free-standing uprights for display purposes; cardboard, scissors, glue, drawing-pins, sellotape, coloured marker pens, cardboard boxes, orange boxes, wood offcuts, rope, string, thin wire, sacking; storage facilities for data (see Chapter 2).

TEACHER PREPARATION

1 You will need to secure a place where your students can erect a shanty house which can be left standing during the period of the project.

2 Contact agencies for information and list resources for the students to follow up, and you will need money for postage and telephone calls.

3 Collect and share magazines, newspapers, etc., for the students to read and abstract information. Note down relevant film, video or radio programmes, which may be useful. Find outside speaker(s).

4 You will need to liaise with the catering services within your school if your students want to organize an austerity lunch.

STUDENT PREPARATION

This will depend on the choice of the objective and whether some of the items listed under *teacher preparation* form part of the actual project from the students' point of view. At this stage the *student preparation* may centre only on reading tasks and selection of information. If the students are going to build the shanty house the collection of the materials can be left to them. You can also ask your students to look out for items in newspapers, or on the radio or TV, relevant to the topic.

ORGANIZATION

1 Decide on timing, e.g. whether data collection is to form part of the project time. Your students can select the areas of interest, e.g. specific countries, health, food, education, political issues, and compile the information from resources available within the classroom or by pursuing their own resources. Arrange a workshop for everyone to survey the materials.

2 Divide the students into pairs or small groups to produce posters and visuals for the display.

3 If your students have decided to organize an austerity lunch or supper, pairs or groups should work on designing the information sheets, publicity handouts, answering some or all of the following questions:
− What is an austerity lunch?
− Why are we having an austerity lunch?
− Where and when? (See Figure 5.3.)

4 Finally, the erection of the shanty house (see Figure 5.4): once built this shanty house is difficult to move so, if possible, build it on its final site where the posters, etc., can be displayed with it, and try to arrange for it to be left in place for a few days, particularly if there will be an austerity lunch as a final event.

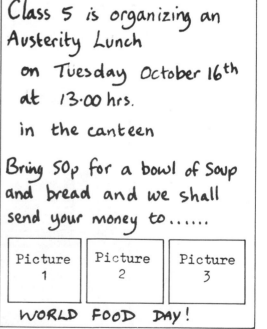

Examples of posters which can be produced by students with text and visuals to be positioned beside shanty house. One group of students shared the same video on malnutrition every day for a week so that all the interested students could have a chance to see it.

Figure 5.3

SKILLS

Reading and related sub-skills; listening skills using video and radio material; note-taking from the radio or TV; summary skills from written materials; using a phone; writing formal letters of request; making plans; giving instructions; use of the imperative; language of persuasion.

FOLLOW-UP

You and your students can organize a fund-raising event for a Third World charity. If you have an austerity lunch or supper, send the donations to the appropriate charity. The students can inform the local newspaper about what the school did to help towards World Food Day. Your students can organize a debate or forum with students from other classes. Note that all charities or agencies acknowledge donations so that these letters of thanks can be displayed.

Build your own

SHANTY HOUSE

The purpose of this sheet is to get you to build a shanty house in a street to attract the attention of passers by: to let them know that what you have built represents the way in which thousands of people live all over the world.

Shanty towns and villages grow up around most of the large cities of South Asia, Latin America and Africa. Shanty houses are mostly too small to house a whole family and its belongings. They have no running water or drainage system and have no protection against the weather. They develop because of the rural drift to the towns. People move from their homes in the country to the city in the hope of finding employment or just a better job. However when they arrive they find that the city can be just as hard a place to find work. As a result they cannot get enough money to buy or rent a proper place to live, and so build their makeshift homes — shanties.

Building a shanty house

The most successful shanty houses are those that make use of the materials that are available locally; a shanty house is exactly what the words say it is. The finished product looks far more effective and consequently more authentic, if it is made from bits of cardboard, plastic sheeting, orange boxes and lengths of wire, rope and string scrounged from local supermarkets and market stalls. The whole idea of such a construction is improvisation, no two shanty houses look the same, either here in this country as a demonstration or in the slums of Buenos Aires. The following notes are meant only to act as a guide and the end result is by no means the answer to a do-it-yourself Shanty House Kit.

Basic Ingredients

½ dozen willing helpers (kidnapped from the local school)
lots of cardboard boxes (scrounged from a local supermarket)
orange boxes   ("   "   "   "   fruit market)
8 (or so) lengths of wood
about 10ft. long   (borrowed from a building site)
bits of wire, rope and string

+ GENEROUS HELPING OF GOOD WEATHER

Figure 5.4

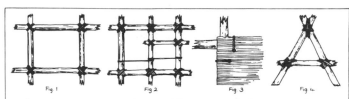

The easiest construction is that of an 'A' frame, although there are several variations to it. Start by laying out on the ground, four pieces of wood in a square format and lash them together using wire (or rope or string) as shown in figure one. Lash onto these other pieces of wood (or bits of plastic or even stretch across bits of rope) making up a crude patchwork arrangement as in figure two. Onto this framework place the cardboard, previously opened and flattened, and by pushing holes in the cardboard, this too can be lashed onto the framework, (figure three).

Having completely covered the framework with cardboard, this now represents one side of the A frame, and the process needs to be repeated for the other side. After completing side two lift them both up and lean together in an inverted V, and lash together. Complete the framework by lashing on support pieces (wood or even metal) to complete the A frame. Cardboard can then be lashed onto one end to complete the house with the entrance at the other.

Variations on a theme

Several variations of the above design are possible. If for instance, materials are scarce it may be possible to lean one side of the A frame against a building as a 'lean to' shanty house or alternatively construct four framework pieces making a rectangular house, putting on a polythene sheet (or cardboard) as a roof.

When the 'shanty' is finished, write on it with felt tip pens, 'Millions of people live in homes like these' etc., or anything relevant to get people passing-by to ask questions about why and what you are doing. Draw up an estate agent's valuation sheet and put it on the house. Write on it such things as: nearest water supply - 2 miles ...... no toilet ...... leaking roof ...... in need of constant repairs etc. ...... no extras.

There are no set rules or instructions for building a shanty house, use your own initiative and most of all have fun.

The shanty house which was built in Nottingham during the National Young Oxfam Conference in April 1978.

Figure 5.4 (continued)

13 Good wheelchair guide

Note that a more detailed discussion of this particular project can be found in *ELT Journal* 36/2: pp. 98–103.

LEVEL

Upper intermediate to Advanced

AGE

Adolescent upwards

TIME

40 hours over 12 weeks

OBJECTIVES

To produce a fact sheet or handbook for disabled people on the facilities available for wheelchairs in the town.

LOCATION

Town or city for fieldwork in the UK. Investigating certain areas, e.g. cinemas, theatres, pubs, restaurants, may entail extra work out of school hours, and you should ensure that your students are willing to give up their spare time voluntarily, and are aware of this extra commitment from the start of the project.

EQUIPMENT

A wheelchair—if possible on loan for the duration of the project. Money for bus fares, telephone calls, entrance fees, petrol if using your own transport. Materials for the end product, i.e. cardboard, spiral binding strips for the handbook, plain paper, photocopying paper; photocopier or gestetner; money for Letraset for headings; typewriters; camera and film (optional); blanket and strap for the student in the wheelchair; notebooks and pens; storage facilities for the data (see Chapter 2).

TEACHER PREPARATION

1 You will have to produce bona fides (see Chapter 2) for your students for their fieldwork. Arrange for the use of a wheelchair.

2 Use a classroom with easy outside access and available out of school hours, evenings, and weekends if required.

3 Arrange for outside speakers, the hire of a video/16 mm film, and a visit to a physically handicapped unit if necessary.

STUDENT PREPARATION

1 If any of your students have direct personal experience of being involved with handicapped people their contributions will be of value during the initial discussions.

2 Ask the students to practise using the wheelchair. If this is to be done off the school premises, check that your students are covered by insurance. The best place to practise using a wheelchair is probably a park.

ORGANIZATION

1 In class the students decide on the target areas for investigation, e.g.
– hotels, guesthouses, restaurants, pubs, cafés
– buses, trains, stations
– museums, galleries

– banks, shops, public toilets, theatres, cinemas, sports centres
– doctors, dentists

2 Having selected the areas, the students work in pairs using the wheelchair (not all the students will want to use the wheelchair). The wheelchair has to be used by the pairs in turn, so the students have to decide exactly what they will want to try out with the wheelchair, and what information can be gained by asking questions on foot.

3 The students draw up a list of places they will cover, and enter the information on a large grid in the classroom, so that everyone can see who is doing what (see Figure 5.5).

SAMPLE GRID

Students	Week 1 11–12 noon	Week 2 3–4 p.m.	Week 3 7–8 p.m.	Week 4 11–12 noon
Victoria and Claire	6 banks in High Street W/C	Check hotel lift doors —widths	Check as many restaurants as possible	Visit sports centre
Sophie and Guy	Station— on foot	3 museums W/C	Check as many restaurants as possible	Check shop doorways
Regula and Thorleif	See City Architect to discuss developments for disabled	Phone guest houses to check facilities	Try three cinemas W/C	Take photos of 'hopeless' and 'ideal' places
Tassy and Yuko	Check pavement heights in city centre	Interview taxi drivers	Try two theatres W/C	Check public toilets W/C

All meet at café at 8 p.m.

Figure 5.5

4 Ensure that the wheelchair changes are made discreetly and away from public view!

5 The students should prepare questions to ask. Organize practice with role play in the class if necessary. They should prepare small maps of the area which they intend to cover, in order to mark ramps, high pavements, accessible toilets, shops, etc.

6 You and your students can discuss the end product, for example, a fact sheet, booklet, etc. They will need to purchase the materials for the end product, e.g. card and spiral binding strips—appropriate because a booklet can then lie flat on a person's knee. During a long-term project such as this one where the information is collected over a period of weeks, I have found that a regular period each week, set aside to focus on the project, works best from the students' point of view, as they are able to organize themselves in advance, and make the most of the time available. As the amount of information grows, it is vital for everyone to see what is being gathered, before individuals or small groups collate the material.

7 The information can then be sub-divided into categories, e.g. restaurants and cafés; banks; entertainment such as cinemas and theatres, etc., with some students collating, probably in the areas they themselves researched, and other students typing up the results, photocopying if a number of copies are going to be produced, and finally inserting them between hard covers and binding. Alternatively, the end result may be a large broadsheet for classroom display only.

8 The development of photographs can be handled by the students themselves if they have the equipment and skills.

SKILLS

All four skills, initially concentrating on reading, listening, and speaking, with note-taking and recording verbatim from interviews at a later stage.

FOLLOW-UP

The follow-up stages to this project will depend on the end product, and the kind of exposure that the group decides upon. If the result is a large classroom broadsheet, students may like to invite fellow students and others to look at the result and to discuss the implications. If fact sheets and/or booklets have been produced, these can be distributed to relevant and interested organizations by the students themselves. Alternatively, a fairly ambitious group may decide to contact the media (see *ELT Journal* article for further discussion), and try to gain publicity through newspapers, magazines, radio, and television. Students working in the UK may contact their own countries and send copies or résumés of the project (in their mother tongue) for publication abroad. The spin-off from this kind of project is considerable, but not predictable.

14 Primary school teaching

LEVEL	**Upper intermediate to Advanced**
AGE	**Young adult upwards** (depending on maturity rather than language level)
TIME	**30 hours over 12 weeks** (at the students' own school or college) **6–8 hours over 8 weeks** (in the primary school)
OBJECTIVES	To establish a working rapport with small groups of children over a long term; to practise the language of instruction in particular; to contribute constructively to a primary school timetable.
LOCATION	A class of children (ideally 7–9 years old) in a local primary school, UK and abroad where English is taught at primary school.
EQUIPMENT	Materials for the students to teach from or with. This is likely to include paper, felt pens, crayons, pictures, glue, scissors, etc., but this cannot be decided before the project starts because it is wholly dependent on the students, therefore the most important item is *extra money*, polaroid or video camera, if available, and transport if the school is not within walking distance.
TEACHER PREPARATION	**1** You will need to negotiate with the primary school and teachers initially, via the head teacher, for approval of the project in general terms. **2** Then you will need to negotiate with the individual class teacher at least a term in advance so that the students' teaching schedule can be included in the overall timetable and curriculum of the primary school. **3** Spend some time with the class in order to familiarize yourself with the school environment.
STUDENT PREPARATION	**1** Initial exposure to the idea of teaching should be discussed in class, with the students using their own primary school experiences, educational objectives, brothers and sisters, and a visit to other primary schools, as well as to the actual school chosen for the project. **2** Some students may like the idea of being involved, while being very apprehensive of actually teaching the children; these students may prefer to involve themselves in the preparation of the teaching materials, and sit in on classes, without actually teaching. **3** The language of instruction will still be rehearsed in the students' classroom and practised during mock sessions.
ORGANIZATION	**1** A visit to the school where your students will ultimately be teaching must take place at least two or three weeks ahead of the first teaching session, so that time is available for the students to prepare the materials.

2 A timetable for student teaching will have to be decided, according to the size of both the student group and the primary class.

3 The students may prefer to divide themselves into small teaching teams based on interests or (in the UK) on nationality. This team-teaching approach works best as it reduces the potential tension of the actual teaching situation, and it may be possible to team confident individuals with less confident ones.

4 A primary school class of 30 or more children needs to be broken down into small groups of 8 to 10 children, and it is best left to the regular class teacher to do this. The students can then produce one set of materials and rotate around the groups, teaching simultaneously.

5 Time has to be allowed for the students to decide on their teaching objectives, to research their materials, to write off for information if necessary, to buy items for their teaching sessions, and to organize small working parties in class. Some examples of what has been done by other students on this project may be helpful:
– Swiss students made a snakes and ladders game which was played on a large pictorial map of Switzerland, with the intention of teaching the children some basic Swiss geography.
– Danish students made a life-size model of a Viking helmet out of papier mâché, in order to talk about the Vikings, and to teach the children how to make a similar helmet.
– Brunei students taught the children how to make and fly the type of kites flown by children in Brunei.
– Thai students taught the children the Thai alphabet so they could write their own names in Thai.
– Japanese students made cartoon strips of a day in the life of a Japanese school child, and showed the children how to do origami.

6 The production of the teaching materials is best organized in workshop sessions. The students can be encouraged to keep a record or a diary of the work as it progresses, and to practise the language they will need, on each other; to try out ideas in advance to see if there are likely to be any practical problems, as in the case of some Brazilian students, who found that the map of Brazil kept falling off their felt board!

7 If the students are going to use a video camera, close-up shots can be tried out in the workshop sessions.

SKILLS

All four skills, in addition to developing student awareness of register and appropriacy in using the language, in relationship with the class teacher, with the children, and with each other. This project highlights the economical use of language which students generally discover for themselves when actually teaching, and which can be usefully exploited in feedback sessions to discuss why the lesson was/was not successful.

FOLLOW-UP

1 One of the greatest spin-offs from this project is the rapid gain in your students' confidence, as they find themselves doing something which they had not even contemplated doing in their mother tongue. It is also a good idea to assemble something tangible at the end of the project. It can be in the form of a report, to which all the students contribute their own experiences, with samples of their materials. This is then displayed for other students to see. Otherwise, a display can be made of the individual diaries, perhaps accompanied by polaroid photographs of the children and their classroom.

2 Once when students did this project, it was decided to use a video camera, primarily to show the children a film of themselves at work. The final version needed editing, and each student wrote his or her own script, and did the voice over. The result, while very rough, caused a sensation, and was greeted with enormous enthusiasm!

3 Students may like to invite the children back to their school or college, and put on an entertainment for them as the culmination to the project.

4 Letters of thanks are likely to be sent, both to the students and also by the students to the school, staff, and children. Establishing a successful relationship with another school can lead to mutual benefit all round.

15 Hospital and spastic unit

LEVEL

Upper intermediate to Advanced

AGE

Young adult/Adult

TIME

Total immersion over 12 weeks (or longer depending on the external facilities available)

OBJECTIVES

To integrate the students into the community through their involvement in a working environment; to provide a basis for a 12 week integrated skills programme.

LOCATION

Outside organization large enough to absorb students who can spend a fixed period of time in the organization, e.g. factory, hospital, old people's home, etc., on a weekly voluntary basis, split up into small groups of three or four. UK or possibly British Forces overseas.

EQUIPMENT

Money for extra materials; audio recording equipment (optional); polaroid camera (optional); video camera (optional); video editing facilities (usually hired) if the video film is to be professionally finished; transport to the institution.

TEACHER PREPARATION

The liaison with outside organizations in order to gain acceptance for a project along these lines can be very time-consuming and protracted, and is best begun at least three months ahead of the envisaged starting point. (The recession in the UK meant that many industries were reluctant to participate, and although it would have been possible to place small groups of students with a number of firms, it would have been difficult to organize and co-ordinate the language programme, because of the diversity of demands and the lack of a total group language need.) This particular case study derives from a project based in a hospital school and spastic unit, both on the same site (although not within comfortable walking distance), and administered by a headmaster with ultimate responsibility for both units. It was anticipated that the students could contribute to the teaching on the wards without too much disruption, catering for both short-stay and long-stay children. Some of the students would contribute to the work of the spastic unit by making a video film on the work of the unit, which could be shown to prospective parents. These objectives, however, were defined by the students, together with the teaching staff, after initial meetings, although approval for the students to participate in one form or another had been agreed in the previous term.

The timetable for visits had also been worked out the previous term, in order to fit in with the internal arrangements of the hospital and spastic unit. The headmaster made various books available to the students for the duration of the project—medical texts dealing with spasticity and other handicaps. It is likely that the head of an organization will be instrumental in ensuring how welcome students feel, and how effective the liaison is between the workers, staff, personnel and visiting students. A project of this nature should not be undertaken without the support of the authorities, as their role is crucial.

STUDENT PREPARATION

1 A visit should be arranged to the organization or institution for observation, time to discuss, gain confidence, meet people, etc.

2 Time should be spent in the classroom to explore the possibilities of a project on these lines, which should only be undertaken by a group able to handle the personal commitment expected by the external organization.

ORGANIZATION

1 With this type of project the organization of work inside and outside the classroom eventually takes on a pattern, centred on the session each week when the students are working outside.

2 The language work becomes dovetailed to fit the students' needs, as each week their experience is extended, and they anticipate coping with a fresh set of circumstances. For example, during one project of this kind, the students felt that they wanted to meet the people with whom they were working, *outside* the working environment. In the end they issued invitations to a supper which they organized and ran themselves. Apart from the practicalities which had to be dealt with, they needed to acquire new language skills which would enable them

to play hosts to a large number of people, to introduce their own teachers to complete strangers, to make a vote of thanks, to offer food and drink, and to sustain all this in a foreign language for a number of hours. The potential for language development was enormous, and the sense of achievement after the event equally so!

3 As this type of project is very clearly outside any control of the teacher, the start of the project must provide time for the students to meet, liaise and receive help, advice and suggestions from the staff of the institution as to how they might best contribute. For the staff of the organization this can be very demanding, as it imposes on their normal working day, and once again it is vital to make these arrangements well in advance to avoid any friction.

4 When dealing with such a wide range of people, it would be naive to suggest that all the students will be welcome by everyone all of the time. It is wise to prepare your students for situations where they might meet resentment, and to work on the kinds of social gambits we employ when faced with hostile reactions. It may also be that the backlash affects the teacher in charge of the group rather than the students, which adds a new dimension to the teacher's role.

SKILLS

All four skills, integrated towards one objective, and the potential for covering a whole range of sub-skills, e.g. writing a formal letter of thanks after the initial visit; exchanging small talk with the native speakers during a tea break; written case studies and diaries of experiences; case histories of individuals within the organization, based on interviews.

FOLLOW-UP

1 Students working on this kind of project have found that informal contacts begin to emerge where they have become emotionally involved with people. This can have obvious drawbacks but is more often a positive advantage.

2 If students are keeping case histories or diaries, the written work is a valuable record of both the experience and the individual student's language development. With the student's consent, these diaries can be exchanged and read by other people, and even passed back to the staff at the institution.

3 If students have set out to make a video, then a video script has to be prepared frame by frame, and the whole group has to work on a commentary acceptable to everyone. In the case of this particular project, the video film was edited professionally (with all the students), and then shown to the children and staff, which gave everyone involved a high degree of satisfaction. Then a copy was handed over to the spastic unit, and each student took a copy home when they left the UK.

4 Figure 5.6 shows the frame by frame video programme used with this particular project, and is followed by part of the script on the project, written by the students.

VIDEO PROGRAMME SCRIPT DONE BY STUDENTS

FRAME	TEXT
1 Project notice	SOT Music
2 Weston Road	SOT Music
3 Bell School sign	One of the houses on Weston Road in Bath is the Bell School of Languages. Here foreign students from all over the world come to learn English.
4 Door—door open	This winter term, which is from January till March 1983, a group of students has been involved in making a project with children at the Bath and Wessex Hospital School, and the spastic unit, The Cynthia Mossman House.
5 Students exit	FU and VO The students concerned are: Abdullah from Turkey Tere from Mexico Madeleine from Switzerland Gunilla from Holland
6 Students board bus	FU and VO Sascha and Stephen from Germany and Ana Lucia from Brazil.
7 Minibus leaves	VO During the term every Wednesday morning was spent at the school and the hospital.
8 Sign RUH	VO The group was divided into two smaller groups. A.T.M.G. chose to teach the children in the hospital wards.
9 Greeting Mr Lewis	FU
10 A.T.M.G. entering the hospital	A. and T. taught different children every time because there was a rapid changeover in those wards. M. and G. both had one child whom they taught for eight weeks. All greeting Mr Lewis.
11 Sign Spastic Unit	VO The other part of the group which means Sascha, Stephan and Ana Lucia chose to make a video film about the children in the Spastic Unit.
12 S.S.A.L. greeting	FU and VO For as long as the term lasted they filmed a complete day in the school, looking at the four classes from the age of 4 to 11.
13 S.S.A.L. entering the school	FU
KEY	SOT Sound on tape FU Fade up sound on tape CS Close shot VO Voice over

Figure 5.6

Student report on the project

. . . the rest of our group is set down at Cynthia Mossman House, the Spastic School in Bath, to make a film about the teaching of spastic children.

The Spastic School of Bath, attached to the Bath Spastic Society, was founded in September 1973 aiming to organize a special school for the twenty handicapped children who were about to leave the physiotherapy treatment which took place at the same building.

Working hard through the years, today the school has about twenty-nine children. They are divided into four classes with about seven to eight pupils in each class, with a teacher and a teacher's assistant. That means one instructor for every four children. This arrangement is specially made in order to concentrate more attention and care on each child to an extent that allows them to be treated as individuals— because no two spastic disabilities are alike, each spastic child has different problems and asks for individual treatment to overcome his or her personal handicap.

The school tries to work with modern and efficient equipment like this simple pencil holder which allows children who can't control their movements to draw and to write more accurately.

Another interesting example of special equipment is this computer called a Possum which was designed to enable physically or mentally handicapped children to identify and compare objects and to learn fundamental counting and reading. The drawing lit up on the left hand side of the board is chosen by the computer. On the right hand side of the board, the child has to move the light to the matching response cell by pressing sensitive handles. Here the child has to find the correct name that fits the illuminated drawing.

The installation of that computer was a great improvement in spastic teaching methods. Formerly, the teaching speed was severely limited by the lack of control in the child's hand movements, specially in writing and number work. With the Possum computer, however, spelling can be learnt much more easily.

Some children are even encouraged to type on an electric typewriter. For most spastic children this is the only way to learn spelling and writing fluently.

Another great difficulty for spastic children, especially if they are dependent on a wheelchair, is the ability to be in contact with nature. The teachers solved this problem by bringing live animals into the classroom. The children look after the animals and so learn. To consolidate this knowledge, the animals become part of the lessons themselves like here, the rabbit Spotty.

In order to integrate spastic children step-by-step into the so-called normal world, they do many activities like going to the theatre and to the zoo as well as horse riding, swimming, and watching educational programmes on TV.

Besides the special treatment for spastic handicaps, the daily life in the spastic school does not differ much from other schools as one might have thought. Certainly, movement control handicaps are very typical of spastic disability, and make children sometimes look strange and unusual, but that doesn't mean that these children are not able to work or to study.

And even if the brain is affected by spasticity, children are still entirely able to discern between love and hate, and to feel hope and despair, boredom and joy. Natural treatment is therefore important in spastic teaching. Only support without prejudice can give the spastic children the necessary confidence in their abilities to overcome their handicaps.

Here two children are taught the use of the electric wheelchair, because they will never be able to walk properly. They are encouraged to have fun with their chairs—and they do; the same as these children.

We, the film team, really enjoyed filming those sequences and after a time we felt very affectionate towards the children. They liked us and we liked them . . . The whole experience will remain very memorable for us all.

Appendix I

The following pages are designed to act as a personal resources unit largely, but by no means exclusively, for teachers in a non-English-speaking environment. For these teachers the facility to research and amass background information for their projects will depend on quick and easy access to addresses, telephone numbers and other contacts. Even if teachers do not feel the need to compile these details, the categories (listed alphabetically) may in themselves suggest potential project areas. In addition to teachers compiling their own index for their own use, the index can also be used by the students undertaking the project, particularly where the initial information-gathering forms part of the actual project, and is not something done by the teacher in advance of the group decision to pursue the project. Maintaining the index so that it remains up-to-date need not be too time-consuming if the index is used regularly, and certainly not as time-consuming as tracking down references from scratch. Where the address and telephone number are of international relevance, e.g. FAO, BBC External Services, these details have already been supplied; there is also a blank section at the end for teachers to add their own sources as they encounter them. Teachers or students writing off for information should always include a self-addressed envelope for the reply—this makes a reply more likely. If the letter is sent abroad, an international reply coupon should be enclosed. Otherwise the envelope should be stamped. Remember to have sufficient postage if anything heavier than a letter is expected in the reply.

You may make photocopies of these pages for classroom use (but please note that copyright law does not normally permit multiple copying of published material).

Personal resources index

Reference   *Address*

Advertising Agencies
For publicity mailing and information about
forthcoming events.

Airports
Large international airports form a catchment
area of English-speaking people in transit, as
well as other sources of the English language
in spoken and written forms.

Art Galleries
Art galleries may have exhibitions of work by
English-speaking artists with back-up
publicity material in English.

Banks
Large banks employ either native speakers of
English or English-speaking personnel,
especially in popular tourist areas.

British or American Forces overseas
B.F.P.O./American F.P.O.
Residential areas, schools and hospitals with
English-speaking personnel/inhabitants.

British Council Offices
Usually located in large cities and offering a
wide range of facilities and contacts, advice
and information.

Public Relations Dept., The British Council,
10 Spring Gardens, London SW1A 2BN,
England, Tel: (01) 930 8466

Bus and Coach Terminals
Within tourist destinations these have
English-speaking people in transit.

Conferences
International conferences held in major towns
and cities provide a source of English-
speaking people; contact the conference
organizers to establish whether
formal/informal access is possible.

Churches
Some churches, such as The English Church in Funchal, Madeira, will attract English-speaking people, as well as providing literature in English.

Embassies
Most embassies will employ English-speaking staff; contact the cultural attaché.

Hotels
Large international hotels have English-speaking employees, and are a source of literature written in English, and English-speaking visitors, etc.

International Relief Agencies

Oxfam — 274 Banbury Road, Oxford OX2 7DZ, England, Tel: (0865) 56777

Save the Children Fund — 157 Clapham Road, London SW9, England, Tel: (01) 582 1414

International Red Cross — 17 Avenue de la Paix, CH 1211 Geneva, Switzerland, Tel: (22) 34 60 01

U.N.I.C.E.F. — Geneva Headquarters, Palais de Nations, CH 1211 Geneva 10, Switzerland, Tel: (22) 98 58 50

Red Crescent — c/o L.O.R.C.S., Chemin des Crets 17, Petit Saconnex CP 276, CH 1211 Geneva, Switzerland, Tel: (22) 34 55 80

Food and Agriculture Organization — Via delle Terme di Caracalla, 00100 Rome, Italy, Tel: (6) 5797

Contact the headquarters for publicity information; many magazines are also a useful source of material, especially *New Internationalist*, subscription enquiries: — New Internationalist, 374 Wandsworth Road, London SW8 4TE, England, Tel: (01) 720 9314

International Sports Events
Contact the organizers to establish whether informal access to English-speaking competitors is possible.

Large Departmental Stores
e.g. Migros, Knopf, Galeries Lafayette, Printemps, etc. Stores catering for tourists employ English-speaking staff and are patronized by English-speaking visitors.

Motoring Organizations
Each country has its own motoring
organization to provide assistance for the
international traveller; most of these
organizations employ some English-speaking
staff.

Museums
Large museums employ English-speaking
personnel, and may publish information in
English.

Multi-National Organizations
e.g. IBM, Phillips, etc.
All major companies employ English-
speaking staff and produce literature in
English; contact the public relations officer.

Post Offices
In city centres in tourist areas large post
offices cater for English-speaking visitors so
that either English-speaking staff or tourists
can be found there.

Restaurants
Restaurants in popular areas may provide
menus in English, employ English-speaking
staff and attract speakers of English.

Radio and Television Stations
Contact the public relations officer to enquire
about a possible visit, and whether English-
speaking staff are available. BBC External
Services broadcast all over the world and
teachers can get details of programmes, times
and wavelengths from the BBC.
(Ask for monthly bulletin entitled *London
Calling*.)

BBC External Services, PO Box 76,
Bush House, London WC2B 4PH, England,
Tel: (01) 240 3456

Seed Merchants
Note that certain countries require import
permits; teachers should check their own
countries' plant quarantine regulations over
seeds. Details in English on general
conditions from:

Ministry of Agriculture, Fisheries and Food,
Great Westminster House, Horseferry Road,
London SW1P 2AE, Tel: (01) 216 6174

Ships
Teachers living near large ports can enquire
from the port authorities when ships are due
to dock—both freight and passenger; in some
cases temporary boarding passes are available
and there are English-speaking passengers
and crew on board.

Railway Stations
All major railway stations cater for English-
speaking passengers and have English-
speaking people in transit.

Trade Exhibitions
These exhibitions attract speakers of
English—both exhibitors and visitors.

Travel Agents
These organizations are a source of publicity
information written in English, as well as
often employing English-speaking staff.

Tourist Offices, Sites and Attractions
These offices will always cater for speakers of
English, and the various tourist attractions
provide access to speakers of English.

Theatres and Concert Halls
English-speaking companies on tour as well as
English-speaking visitors may provide
occasional sources of contact with the
language.

School Exchange Schemes
Some schools operate exchange programmes
and penfriend schemes; teachers should
contact their local education authority to
investigate establishing such links, if they do
not already exist.

Twinned Towns
Teachers should approach their local council
offices to discover whether their own town is
twinned with a town in the UK; such links
provide a variety of ways for furthering
language contacts.

Universities
Most universities will have a department
where English is taught; these departments
can be approached with a view to
formal/informal contacts with the teaching
staff and their families, especially any
expatriate staff working there.

Youth Hostels
This organization is international and many
speakers of English use the facilities. Your
own country will almost certainly have an
affiliated organization.

Fill in your own entries here:

(UK headquarters)

Y.H.A., 14 Southampton Street, London
WC2, England, Tel: (01) 240 3158

Appendix II

The purpose of this appendix is to make teachers aware of the kinds of project work already being undertaken outside the UK by teachers of English for whom English is a second language. Many of these teachers have instinctively adopted a project-work approach; references to their work are included here in conjunction with their own comments where appropriate.

Belgium

Teachers in Bruges teaching 12 and 13-year-old students have organized project work (after approximately 55 hours' teaching) on the theme of 'English Afternoon Tea'. Their approach involves reading and discussion on an aspect of English culture, and they have chosen to focus on the traditional English tea-time. The teachers exploit the idea further by, for example, producing recipes for scones; the students write out shopping lists in order to buy the ingredients, and actually make the scones. The fact that they use their mother tongue to purchase the items does not detract from the impetus behind the project. Once they have made the scones, they can entertain their friends from other classes by running a café in the classroom, carrying out their roles of serving, taking orders, etc., in English.

Brazil

At the Catholic University of São Paulo a lecturer at the university has organized 'Projects in English' for students to carry out research in their own topic areas. A detailed discussion of her methodology, entitled 'Acquiring English Through Projects', can be found in *World Language English*, Vol. 3, No. 3, pp. 164–7, 1984.

Finland

In Helsinki and Porvoo teachers in both schools and colleges have used project work as a means of preparing their students to cope with what they call 'street English', i.e. authentic English encountered outside the classroom. Teachers have made use of visitors to Helsinki both formally and informally. For example, at the Commercial Exhibition of the European Nuclear Medicine Congress, the Finlandia Hall in Helsinki and the surrounding concourse was full of people coming and going and conducting their exchanges in English. A simple project set up along the lines of either *Street interviews* or *String and pin display* described in *Case studies* (Chapter 5), involved stopping people and asking them where they came from, whether they were enjoying themselves, and whether they liked Helsinki.

Another teacher made use of an English friend working in Finland. She organized a project which started with language work in the classroom and ended with an excursion into Helsinki. Unknown to her students, however, she arranged for her friend to waylay them in the street. '. . . I have laid out a scheme arranging for a friend of mine, an English person, to meet us in a definite place in the street and approach my students and ask for the way, ask about the way to the Houses of Parliament, for instance, or some other place. And then they will have a chance to give him some practical advice about how to get to this place.' Invariably the students offer to take the visitor there, so he is temporarily adopted by the unsuspecting students who are excited by the apparently fortuitous opportunity of practising their English. It is also interesting to note that Finnish teachers, like their Belgian colleagues, have exploited an English tea-shop project. '. . . they prepare the food at home and bring it back to school. Then we serve original English cream tea with jam and toast and things like that . . . very few Finns know what a cream tea is, as a matter of fact!'

Finnish teachers have also made contact with visiting theatre groups and asked actors and actresses to visit their school or college in order to talk about the production, their profession, etc., and to answer students' questions.

Germany

In Hessen, secondary school teachers of English have developed project work along a variety of lines; they have prepared students to make a video cassette depicting various aspects of German life, for exchange with an American school. At other schools, American soldiers from nearby bases have been invited to join students in Christmas activities. On other projects, students interview foreigners working in Germany whom they encounter during their six weeks' *Berufs Praktikum* (work experience) in the ninth form. Some teachers have based projects on the production of a newspaper in English, the collection of labels with English names from all kinds of products, and in one school a 4–6 week project integrated a variety of activities— play-reading, cooking, watching films, performing short plays to culminate in an English Day.

In Bremerhaven another project entitled *Mini-Project Peace* has involved collaboration with Danish teachers. This project was undertaken with students in the tenth form and initially involved them in collecting as much authentic material as was available on the theme of peace, such as, songs, comics, films, articles, books, magazines, brochures, posters, etc. Arising out of this impetus students then went on to discuss the significance and ideas behind the concept, and explored the language needed to prepare for interviews and discussions with visiting speakers. They also displayed their materials, and produced a Disarmament Calendar with each month of the year focussing on a different aspect of the theme of peace, ranging from songs, poetry, games, and visuals.

Italy

In Gubbio, Italian teachers have developed a number of projects with their students. 'All of the students engaged in projects up to now have had to their credit about two years' worth of a basic English Language course (approx. 180 hours) taught through a communicative approach within a state school or, in addition to this, another year's course of ELT with heavy project-work emphasis.' In some cases, mother-tongue subject teachers and foreign-language teachers have worked together to develop integrated project activities. Figure II.1 gives details of three of the projects undertaken. L_2 and L_1, in the cases illustrated in Figure II.1 are English and Italian. (It is worth noting

Project type	Users of project outcome	Field of research for project activity	Average initial L_2 competence level of students	Examples of projects carried out	Quantity of L_2/L_1 use
1	L_2—speaking categories only (e.g. visiting English/American students; other English-speaking visitors)	something in the L_1 context	lower intermediate	—hosting a group of Eng./Amer. students for 1/2 weeks: planning school+ recreational activities; providing hospitality; organizing and guiding tours to places of interest in the area; writing up fact-sheets on/mini-guides to the town (Gubbio, Italy)	L_2 mostly; some L_1 integration in research phase (Art/History/ Games) L_2 end product
2	L_2—speaking catergories+ L_1—speaking categories (e.g. visitors; tourists local inhabitants)	something in the L_1 context	intermediate lower intermediate	—the production of a bilingual guide to folk festivals in the Province of Perugia —the study of disappearing medieval crafts in Gubbio's historic setting, with the production of L_1 and L_2 copies of a tourist brochure on the topic, the setting up of an exhibit and guided L_1 and L_2 tours on various craft itineraries	L_2 and L_1 integration throughout L_2 end product L_1 end product
3	the students themselves (L_1—speaking, L_2—learning)	something in the L_2 context	lower intermediate intermediate upper intermed./ advanced	—establishing a school link with an English school; organizing a class exchange trip to England as a result of the link; planning the class's stay (itinerary, etc.) —preparing resource materials (group dossiers) on ways to approach and analyse different types of texts/materials in L_2 —following through an important news event (the American Presidential election campaign) in the L_1 media and English language printed media (with interviews to American Embassy Reps.), for a school report on the event, with an analysis of the election outcome (L_2), and an article for the local town newspaper (L_1)	L_2 only throughout +for end product (authentic materials, sources and contacts) L_2+some L_1 integration L_2 end product L_1 end product

Figure II.1

that Belgian and Norwegian teachers have also developed projects based on establishing links with English and American schools; in some instances these links are extended with visits—for which some of the preparation is organized by their students.)

Norway

In Bergen, Norwegian teachers have specialized in project work during the summer months when tourists visit the city. The teachers and their students 'prepare questions in the class to put to tourists, it depends on the stage, of course, the pupils are at—if it's beginners you put some easy questions, you make up some easy questions: "where d'you come from?", "d'you like Norway?"—that kind of thing, and well, of course, the pupils have to introduce themselves first and say what they're doing. . . . And with intermediate and advanced students you put them into groups and they prepare the questions themselves according to what sort of information they would like to have from the foreigners visiting our city. . . . Then if it's groups of course, you have them try out what they do, using a cassette recorder; then afterwards you swop them with the different groups and of course they're mostly interested in what they've done themselves. Sometimes if they've been lucky with their foreigners, then it works very well and they're interested in what the others have got as well.'

The Norwegian teachers also make use of role-play exercises in the classroom during the preparatory stages of a project, and with more advanced students they take the opportunity to explore areas of emotional reaction, e.g. embarrassment (when faced with an interview situation), which enables their students to practise the language needed to convey hypotheses.

Yugoslavia

In Belgrade, teachers have organized English evenings and used these occasions to involve their students in the planning and presentation of such events. This involves discussing and planning the programme, designing and making posters to advertise the evenings, inviting speakers and visitors to participate in the evenings. In the main these evening programmes cater for adult learners, but afternoon programmes based on such themes as English fairy stories or nursery rhymes and songs have also proved successful.

Bibliography

Breen, M. P.   1982. 'Communicative Language Teaching'. *Teacher Training and the Curriculum*. London: The British Council.

This paper subtitled 'How Would We Recognize a Communicative Language Classroom?' discusses 1. Material Resources within the Classroom, 2. The Learners, 3. The Teacher, 4. The Classroom as a Genuine Resource, and 5. Why 'Communicative?' There is also a short, useful bibliography.

Brotta, F.   1985. 'L_2 project work in L_1 context'. *Problems and Experiences in the Teaching of English*. Volume II, No. 2.

Child Education and Junior Education   Leamington Spa: Scholastic Publications Ltd.
These are monthly publications.

Although ostensibly for primary school teachers teaching native speakers, they provide valuable stimuli and resource material for teachers at other levels, and contain separate features on project-based activities, e.g. zoos, food, etc., with plenty of useful ideas and suggestions which easily lend themselves to the EFL classroom.

Fried-Booth, D. L.   1982. 'Project work with advanced classes'. *ELT Journal*. Volume 36/2: pp. 98–103

This article outlines a full-scale project which focuses on the problems faced by disabled visitors to the city of Bath.

Jones, K.   1982. *Simulations in Language Teaching*. Cambridge: Cambridge University Press.

This book, which is learner-centred in its orientation, covers definition, design, choice, use, and assessment of simulations and includes a useful bibliography.

Jones, K.   1974. *Nine Graded Simulations*. Ampthill: Management Games Ltd.

This series of simulations was formerly published by ILEA and includes *Radio Covingham*.

Legutke, M. and W. Thiel   1983. *Airport: ein Project für der Englischunterricht in Klasse 6*. Hessisches Institut für Bildungsplanung und Schulentwicklung (HIBS), Abt. 1E, Bodenstedstrasse 7, D–6200 Wiesbaden.

This booklet describes the organization of a project based on a visit to Frankfurt airport by secondary students; the booklet contains teachers' notes and learners' materials.

Littlewood, W.   1981. *Communicative Language Teaching*. Cambridge: Cambridge
                          University Press.

                          This book provides an introduction to communicative language
                          teaching for practising classroom teachers. The central part of the
                          book is devoted to methodology and the role of the teacher; it also
                          includes a comprehensive bibliography.

Lynch, M.   1977. *It's Your Choice*. London: Edward Arnold.

                          A series of role-play exercises designed for native speakers in
                          secondary schools, but it can be adapted for foreign speakers. The
                          pack contains six separate topic-based exercises with information in
                          the form of maps, diagrams, reports, and role guidelines set out on
                          eight cards.

Geography Games   1973. Harlow: Longman Group Ltd.

                          This is a pack of sixteen units containing fifteen games and simulations
                          linked to related material; it contains teachers' notes, suggestions for
                          follow-up work, and further references. Although designed for native
                          speakers it can be adapted for EFL purposes.

SAGSET   is the Society for Academic Gaming and Simulation in Education and
                          Training. It has a growing EFL/ESL section and offers resource lists
                          and advice on gaming materials for teaching. Details from: The
                          Secretary, SAGSET, Centre for Extension Studies, University of
                          Technology, Loughborough, LEICS. LE11 3TV.

Sturtridge, G. and D.   1979. *ELT Guide to Simulations*. NFER-Nelson. London: The British
Herbert   Council.

                          This contains examples of techniques for materials design which can
                          be adapted to local teaching situations. The authors briefly discuss the
                          value, stages, and structure of simulation but the core of the book
                          describes four separate simulations in detail.

31 275